communism

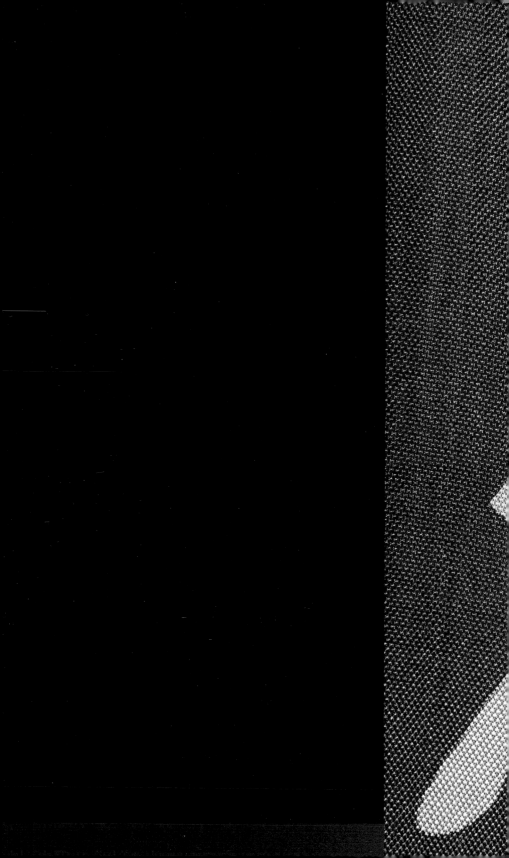

communism

TOM LANSFORD

Marshall Cavendish
Benchmark
New York

Marshall Cavendish Benchmark
99 White Plains Road ▪ Tarrytown, NY
10591 ▪ www.marshallcavendish.us ▪
Copyright © 2008 by Marshall Cavendish
Corporation ▪ Maps Copyright © 2008
by Marshall Cavendish Corporation ▪
Maps by XNR Productions Inc. ▪ All
rights reserved. No part of this book may
be reproduced or utilized in any form or
by any means electronic or mechanical
including photocopying, recording, or
by any information storage and retrieval
system, without permission from the
copyright holders. ▪ All Internet sites
were available and accurate when sent to
press. ▪ Lansford, Tom. ▪ Communism
/ by Tom Lansford. ▪ p. cm. — (Political
systems of the world) ▪ Summary:
"Gives an overview of communism as a
political system, including a historical
discussion of communist regimes
throughout the ▪ world"—Provided by
publisher. ▪ Includes bibliographical
references and index. ▪ ISBN-13: 978-0-
7614-2628-8 ▪ 1. Communism—Juvenile
literature. I. Title. II. Series. ▪ HX73.L35
2007 ▪ 335.43—dc22 ▪ 2007018249

Photo research by Connie Gardner ▪
Cover photo by The Granger Collection ▪
Photographs in this book are used by
permission and through the courtesy
of: The Granger Collection: Back
Cover, 1, 3, 8; Corbis: Bettmann, 13, 25;
Hulton-Deutsch Collection, 35; Reuters,
37; Dmitri Baltermans/The Dmitri
Baltermans, 70; Getty Images: Hulton
Archive, 22, 30; Laski Diffusion, 47;
AFP, 97; AP Photo: Mary Lederhandler,
42; Greg Baker, 78; Stringer, 101, 106,
107; The Image Works: Mary Evans
Picture Library, 61; Kurt B. SV/
Bilderdienst, 89 ▪
Publisher: Michelle Bisson ▪
Art Director: Anahid Hamparian ▪
Series Designer: Sonia Chaghatzbanian ▪
Printed in Malaysia ▪
1 3 5 6 4 2

WITH THANKS TO ZOLTAN BARANY,
FRANK C. ERWIN JR. PROFESSOR IN
THE DEPARTMENT OF GOVERNMENT
AT THE UNIVERSITY OF TEXAS,
FOR HIS EXPERT REVIEW OF THIS
MANUSCRIPT.

Contents

communism

The Elements of Communism 1

COMMUNISM IS A POLITICAL, SOCIAL, AND ECONOMIC system in which the government is based on a collective society with land, property, and economic activities controlled by the state. It was originally conceived as a way to improve the lives and opportunities of the poor. Communism is the opposite of free-market capitalism. Communists believe that the basis for inequality in the world is class struggle: the wealthy class (commonly referred to as the "bourgeoisie") attempts to exploit the working poor (the "proletariat"). The ultimate goal of communism is to create a society in which everyone is equal and there are no social or economic classes. In order to eliminate the class struggle, the proletariat has to rise up against the bourgeoisie and remove that group's economic and political power. The term communism was first used in 1840 by the English writer John Goodwyn Barmby to describe French groups endeavoring to overthrow their government and create a classless society.

The ideals of communism were never achieved. Writing in the 1960s, the scholar Robert Daniels noted that "Communism is grounded in illusion." Many of the basic components of the original system were altered and revised by regimes during the twentieth century. As a result, there has never been a true communist government, only a succession of regimes that claimed to be communist and that incorporated some aspects of the ideology into political or economic policies. In addition, many communist governments used the basic ideas of the political theory as an excuse to centralize political and economic resources, and to suppress dissent. For instance, all communist governments only allowed one political party, the national Communist Party, to have any real political power. Some regimes did allow other political parties to exist, but they were actually controlled by the state and existed mainly for propaganda value.

Most communist regimes have ruled countries that historically have a large poor population. Communist governments usually come to power following a revolution in which the existing political and social order is overthrown. Examples of this trend include Russia, China, and Cuba. Communism claims to enhance the quality of life of the poorest of the poor. When communists come to power, the accumulated wealth and land of the bourgeoisie is expropriated by the regime and used to improve the lives and status of the proletariat through new social and economic opportunities. On the other hand, many communist regimes were installed as the result of conquest. The states of Eastern Europe had communist governments put in place either directly by the Soviet Union, or through Soviet support, in the aftermath of World War II. No communist government ever came to power as the result of free and fair elections. Instead, these regimes were installed by force either through internal revolutions or outside conquest.

Communism was a common form of government throughout most of the twentieth century. By the mid–1980s, one-third of the world's people lived under this form of government. However, by the twenty-first century, only a small number of communist countries survived, representing less than one-quarter of the population. The decline of communism was caused by governments' inability to achieve the ideals of the system and tendency to become totalitarian regimes.

THE PRINCIPLES OF COMMUNISM

Communist governments usually claim to be based on five main principles, although no regime ever successfully implemented the principles. First, the government owns all businesses and controls the economy. For example, factories are not owned by private citizens or corporations, but are the property of the state. Workers are employed directly by the government, which determines wages, products, and services, as well as production levels. This also means that the government usually decides the occupation of workers based on the skills of the individual and needs of society at the time. The government also oversees all long-range economic planning. Common among communist regimes are five- and ten-year economic plans that set specific targets for economic growth, the production of commodities and products, and wages. Therefore, the economy operates on the basis of government goals rather than consumer preferences or the law of supply and demand. These plans lead to economies that are highly rigid and often unable to react to change, caused by economic problems such as drought or famine or societal shifts such as sudden increases or decreases in population.

Second, there is no real estate. Instead, land is owned by the government, which is supposed to ensure that any benefits or profits from the land are distributed equally throughout society. For instance, in communist countries, there are no individual or family farms; instead, people work in large agricultural units known as collective farms. The profits from the crops and livestock produced on these collectives are taken by the government to help pay for services such as health care and education. Also, because there is no private land, there is no right of inheritance. Most people live in their homes under lifetime leases. When they die, the government takes control of their homes. No private property also means that people typically do not own their homes or apartments. Instead they pay rent or have housing provided free.

Third, government control of wages creates, again only in theory, a classless society in which there are no rich or poor. Instead, everyone is more or less equal in political, social, and economic terms. In the United States and most Western industrialized countries, society is often described as consisting of three classes: the rich, the middle class, and the poor. Ideally, the middle class is the largest segment of the population. However, in many communist countries, the poor are the largest segment of the population, easily outnumbering the rich and middle class combined. For example, in Russia before the Revolution in 1917, the combined rich and middle class made up less than 10 percent of the total population. Communists say that capitalist societies have only two classes: rich and poor, or bourgeoisie and proletariat. They combine the rich and middle class into one category. In order for communism to be implemented, the bourgeoisie have to be eliminated. The result would be a classless society in which everyone is equal since the wealth of the bourgeoisie would be redistributed to the poor.

The Communist Manifesto (1848)

The *Communist Manifesto* was written by Karl Marx and Friedrich Engels. The document serves as the basis for the ideology of communism. In the *Manifesto* the authors describe their view of the class struggle:

> The history of all hitherto existing society is the history of class struggles.
>
> Freeman and slave, patrician and plebeian, lord and serf, guild-master and journeyman, in a word, oppressor and oppressed, stood in constant opposition to one another, carried on an uninterrupted, now hidden, now open fight, a fight that each time ended, either in a revolutionary reconstitution of society at large, or in the common ruin of the contending classes.
>
> In the earlier epochs of history, we find almost everywhere a complicated arrangement of society into various orders, a manifold gradation of social rank. In ancient Rome we have patricians, knights, plebeians, slaves; in the Middle Ages, feudal lords, vassals, guild-masters, journeymen, apprentices, serfs; in almost all of these classes, again, subordinate gradations.
>
> The modern bourgeois society that has sprouted from the ruins of feudal society has not done away with class antagonisms. It has but established new classes, new conditions of oppression, new forms of struggle in place of the old ones.

Our epoch, the epoch of the bourgeoisie, possesses, however, this distinct feature: it has simplified class antagonisms. Society as a whole is more and more splitting up into two great hostile camps, into two great classes directly facing each other—Bourgeoisie and Proletariat.

Fourth, social welfare benefits, such as education, health care, and retirement pensions, are available to all citizens free of charge. During the twentieth century, communist states clamed some of the highest literacy rates in the world. In addition, these regimes usually had highly developed and well-funded medical systems (this was especially true of the communist states of Eastern Europe). Nonetheless, medical care was often below the quality standard in Western Europe or the United States. This was especially true for women and marginalized groups in society.

Fifth, all contemporary communist governments are totalitarian regimes that limit political expression and dissent. Communist states also tend to abolish or limit religion and religious practices in order to prevent alternative beliefs from competing with communist ideology. Governments typically justify such repression on the grounds that alternative political ideologies would slow the development of a classless society. One result of this trend in the twentieth century was longstanding conflict with the noncommunist world. Western governments, including the United States, initially refused to recognize the communist governments in countries such as the Soviet Union and China. Communist governments openly asserted a goal of world domination in order to finally achieve a truly classless world society.

MARXISM

Forms of communism have been around throughout human history. Modern communism is based on the political and economic theories of Karl Marx, a nineteenth-century German intellectual. He wrote several books with his friend and collaborator, Friedrich Engels, which formed the foundation for communism. Both Marx and Engels were socialists: they believed that private property caused inequality in society and that governments should control their nation's economy so that the basic needs of people could be satisfied. During the Industrial Revolution in Europe, there were great disparities between the rich and poor. Factory owners and merchants grew very rich because the use of machinery to make new products and provide services reduced the value of workers. Machines did more work and replaced the labor that had been provided by people. Over time, there were more workers than jobs. Owners and managers began to pay their employees less because it was easy to replace them. The result was widespread poverty, even among workers. This group of working poor lived mainly in the cities and were referred to as the working class. While the working class lived in squalor and poverty, business owners and investors grew richer because machines meant that it cost less to make their products. Marx and Engels sought to develop a political ideology that would reduce poverty and inequality. The result was communism, an egalitarian political and economic system.

The communist governments of the twentieth and twenty-first centuries are loosely based on Marxism, which combines the main principles of communist government with Marx's own sweeping and complex vision of history. Marx believed that history was marked by constant strife and class warfare. He based his theory on the work of German philosopher George W. F. Hegel (1770–1831). Hegel argued that every idea (the "thesis") was immediately challenged by its opposite (the "antithesis"). For instance, Christianity was challenged by atheism. Eventually, the two opposing concepts would blend into a combination known as the synthesis. However, that synthesis would then be challenged by its opposite and reignite the conflict between thesis and antithesis. Hegel termed this conflict of ideas as the dialectic.

Marx used Hegel's concept of the dialectic but added his own twist: he argued that the conflict between the bourgeoisie (the thesis) and the proletariat (the antithesis) could produce a final synthesis in the form of a perfectly classless egalitarian society. This society could only be achieved following a workers' revolution that would dislodge the existing power structure. Such a conflict would occur only in countries that were industrialized with wide gaps between the rich and poor. Marxists tend to focus on the existence of class warfare and the need for revolution. One of the main flaws of Marx's work is that he did not develop a formal governmental system. Instead, most of his writing dealt with the theoretical causes of class conflict and the need for revolution. Later intellectual figures would fill in the gaps in Marxist ideology.

Karl Marx
(1818–1883)

Karl Marx is commonly referred to as the "father" of communism. Marx was born on May 5, 1818, in Trier, Germany, to a Jewish family. Marx's father, a lawyer, later converted to Lutheranism since Jews were not allowed to practice law in Germany at the time. An intelligent and gifted youth, Marx earned a doctorate from the University of Jena in 1841. He became well-known for his opposition to the aristocracy and his promotion of political equality. Marx was appointed editor of a radical antigovernment journal after graduation. He married in 1843, but he and his family were forced to leave Germany after the government suspended publication of the journal. Marx moved to Paris, where he began to collaborate with his lifelong friend Friedrich Engels. Because of his revolutionary ideas, Marx was banished from France in 1845 and moved to Brussels, Belgium.

In 1847, Marx and Engels established the Communist League. In 1848, they wrote *The Communist Manifesto,* one of the earliest works about communism. In that short piece, Marx and Engels advocated the use of violence to implement their ideals. This led to Marx's exile from Belgium. He and his family settled in London, where he remained for the rest of his life. Marx helped found the International Working Men's Association (the First International) in 1864. This group sought to unite all workers to overthrow the existing economic system and replace it with a socialist system. While in London, Marx also worked strenuously on his magnum opus, *The Capital: A Critique of Political Economy* (commonly known by its German title, *Das Kapital*). While the majority of the ideas and work in *Das Kapital* are Marx's, he died on March 14, 1883, before the manuscript was complete. Engels finished and edited the two-volume work which presented Marx's ideology, known as Marxism, and became the basis for modern communism.

Marxism-Leninism

Vladimir Ilyich Lenin (1870–1924) led the communist revolution that took power in Russia in 1917. Lenin translated Marx's theories into a governing system that came to be known as Marxism-Leninism. For instance, Marx predicted that worker revolutions would sweep through Europe, but by 1900 this had not occurred. Lenin claimed that imperialism delayed the onset of revolution because countries were able to exploit poorer countries to aid their economies and keep prices down. Workers were satisfied and their quality of life actually improved due to inexpensive imported goods. Lenin further asserted that large international corporations within the imperialist countries formed monopolies on certain products or services and then divided the world economy between them. These monopolies actually eliminated competition within the international economy and Lenin correctly predicted they would ultimately lead to higher prices and less choice. Lenin's interpretation of imperialism differed from Marx's. He argued that communist revolutions were most likely to occur in the developing world and not in the industrial societies of Western Europe because of the relatively high standard of living of those countries. Lenin believed that as revolutions were successful in the developing world, they would spread to the richer countries. Like Marx, though, Lenin argued that communism could only be successful if it spread across the globe.

Lenin also believed that communism could only succeed if the government was controlled by a single Communist Party. This nondemocratic regime, known as the dictatorship of the proletariat, would serve as a transition from the old, capitalist system to the eventual classless, egalitarian society. In between, society would have to be governed by an oligarchy that consisted of high-ranking members of the Communist Party. Once in power in Russia, Lenin ruthlessly suppressed dissent and worked to spread communism to surrounding countries. After the revolution, the former parts of the Russian empire were joined together to create the Union of Soviet Socialist Republics (USSR), or Soviet Union, a federation of states under the control of the new Russian capital.

Lenin's successor, Joseph Stalin (1878–1953), further refined communist ideology into a system known as Stalinism. Stalin slowly eliminated rivals within the Communist Party through a series of

Vladimir Ilyich Lenin was the first communist leader of the Soviet Union. Here he speaks to a group of workers in Petrograd in 1917.

purges. In the 1930s, some 35,000 Soviet military officers were killed so they would not pose a threat to Stalin's reign and as a warning to any future challengers. In addition, while Lenin had allowed some flexibility in economic planning, Stalin ordered the forced collectivization of farms. The result was a massive famine that resulted in an estimated five to six million deaths. By the late 1930s, Stalin had replaced the party oligarchy with a personal dictatorship. Later Soviet leaders rejected many of Stalin's actions and political control again came to rest on a party oligarchy. Examples of Marxist-Leninist states include the former Soviet Union and the former communist states of Eastern Europe, such as Poland, Hungary, and East Germany. Most of the remaining contemporary communist states, such as Cuba and North Korea, combine Marxism-Leninism with the second main variation of communism: Maoism.

Maoism

The Chinese developed their own form of Marxism, which has come to be known as Maoism, after the first Chinese communist leader, Mao Zedong (1893–1976). Mao combined elements of traditional Chinese culture, including Confucianism, with Marxism. Mao imbued his brand of communism with Chinese nationalism, especially hatred of the colonial powers such as the Europeans and the Japanese who had carved China into spheres of influence. He also sought to develop a "united front" of people from all social classes so that the Chinese communist revolution was not simply a proletarian revolt. Mao's interpretation of Marxism is formally known as "Mao Zedong Thought" and remains the official basis for Chinese communism. Mao communicated his theories through the publication of a short book, *Quotations from Chariman Mao Zedong*. The pocket-sized edition was known in the West as *Chairman Mao's Little Red Book*. The book had quotations and sayings from Mao.

Unlike Marxism-Leninism, Maoism contends that the revolution to overthrow the bourgeoisie can be led by rural peasants and other segments of society (the united front) rather than the proletariat. Mao's ideas were rooted in the Chinese reality in which peasants had installed the communist regime. Mao believed in the importance of organization and saw communist revolutions evolving in stages. Initially, small groups of communists needed to be organized to fight an unconventional insurgency or guerrilla war. Over time, the

Lenin and the Highest Stage of Capitalism

In 1916, Lenin wrote *Imperialism, the Highest Stage of Capitalism,* to explain the relationship between capitalism and imperialism:

> Imperialism emerged as the development and direct continuation of the fundamental characteristics of capitalism in general. But capitalism only became capitalist imperialism at a definite and very high stage of its development, when certain of its fundamental characteristics began to change into their opposites, when the features of the epoch of transition from capitalism to a higher social and economic system had taken shape and revealed themselves all along the line. Economically, the main thing in this process is the displacement of capitalist free competition by capitalist monopoly. Free competition is the fundamental characteristic of capitalism, and of commodity production generally; monopoly is the exact opposite of free competition, but we have seen the latter being transformed into monopoly before our eyes, creating large-scale industry and forcing out small industry, replacing large-scale by still larger-scale industry, and carrying concentration of

production and capital to the point where out of it has grown and is growing monopoly. . . . At the same time the monopolies, which have grown out of free competition, do not eliminate the latter, but exist over it and alongside of it, and thereby give rise to a number of very acute, intense antagonisms, frictions and conflicts.

Mao Zedong was China's first communist leader. Here, communists read from his *Little Red Book* in front of a poster of Mao.

noncommunist government would grow unpopular because of its inability to suppress the rebellion and more and more people would join the insurgency. Once the communists had the support of the majority of the people, the government could be overthrown and a communist regime installed.

Maoism also emphasized that communist regimes faced a continuing threat from the bourgeoisie. Therefore, communist governments had to be constantly vigilant. In China, there were constant purges against elements that could threaten the regime, culminating in a broad campaign known as the Cultural Revolution (1966–1976). During the Cultural Revolution, thousands were arrested and the government attempted to suppress all non-Chinese communist culture and art. Besides China, Maoism was the official policy of states such as Albania, and influenced other communist parties in Latin America and Asia.

Partially in reaction to the Cultural Revolution, China began liberalizing its economy after Mao's death. Under the leadership of Deng Xiaoping (1949–1997), China began to introduce free market reforms. This changed the nature of Chinese communism so that the government focused more on political issues and allowed greater individual economic freedom, including ownership of private property and the accumulation of wealth. Modern Chinese communism has embraced many of the principles that were opposed by traditional Marxism-Leninism and Maoism. The result has been dramatic improvements in the country's economy, but many critics argue that these gains have come at the cost of the traditional benefits of communism, including the social welfare system.

2

History of Communism

COMMUNISM HAS ITS ROOTS IN ANTIQUITY. Early religious figures advocated societies in which wealth and property were shared by the community. Many ancient philosophers believed that if a society was fair and equal, people would treat each other more equitably. There were also political movements in the 1500s and 1600s to abolish private property and there are foreshadowings of communist socialism during the French Revolution in the late eighteenth century. Nonetheless, it was not until Marx and Engels began collaborating in the mid–1800s that communism emerged as a coherent political ideology. Only in the 1900s was communism implemented as the political system for a national government.

COMMUNISM'S ROOTS

In ancient Greece, many of the myths about an earlier golden age were based on the notion of an era when everything was shared and there was no private property. Philosophers such as Plato (427–347 BCE) advocated the creation of communes that emphasized equality. In addition, in *The Republic,* Plato theorized about a class of warriors, the Guardians, who gave up private property and wealth to serve the state. Communal property was also common in some tribes in the Americas and Asia.

Early Christianity had many elements that were later incorporated into communism. The Acts of the Apostles (usually simply known as

Acts, a book of the Bible) describe early Christian sects that practiced communal living, shared property, and rejected wealth. Some Christians later would argue that the teachings of Jesus supported communism as the ideal society because of its goal of equality of wealth. Citations from the gospels of Luke or Matthew lend credence to the notion that Jesus advocated the rejection of private property. For instance, in Matthew 19:24, Jesus is quoted as saying that "It is easier for a camel to go through the eye of a needle, than for a rich man to enter into the kingdom of God." These Christian notions of equality, through the rejection of wealth and status and community ownership of property, were incorporated in the communist ideals of collectivism and shared wealth.

Thomas More of England (1478–1535) wrote about an ideal society that was basically communistic in his book, *Utopia*. Furthermore, during the English Civil Wars (1642–1651), a group known as the "Diggers," or the "True Levelers," espoused a doctrine that included agricultural reform and the redistribution of land and communal ownership. Such sentiments led to the development of a contemporary philosophy known as Christian communism in the late 1800s in England that combined elements of modern communism with Christianity. Christian communists reject the notion of armed revolution, but embrace the communist ideals of collective property and a classless society.

Utopians and Socialists
In addition to More, other philosophers developed theories about the problems of private property and the benefits of communal societies. Enlightenment thinkers such as French philosopher Jean-Jacques Rousseau (1712–1778) and Immanuel Kant (1724–1804) of Germany argued against private property because of the inequalities that occurred when individuals or families acquired large tracts of land. Other philosphers wrote about ideal societies in which property and wealth were shared by all citizens. These idealists were collectively known as the Utopians. Perhaps the most prominent Utopian was the English mill owner Robert Owen (1771–1853). Owen incorporated the concepts of socialism into a series of communes, among them New Lanark, England, and New Harmony, Indiana, in the United States. Owen believed that small communities of 1,000 to 2,000 people could live in harmony without private property. Owen's ideas did not gain widespread acceptance, but they did influence later communist thinkers. Other Utopian communes were formed, including one in Clayon County,

Illinois, in the 1800s. A prominent communal settlement in Paris was led by Claude-Henri de Rouvroy Saint-Simon (1760–1825), who is often regarded as the father of modern socialism.

Saint-Simon emphasized collective ownership, but did not believe in the elimination of classes, although he advocated equality across class lines. Other early socialists included the Frenchman Charles Fourier (1772–1837) whose ideals led to the creation of a socialist commune at Brook Farm in Massachusetts in the 1840s.

Socialism significantly influenced communism and many of the themes of early socialist thinkers were incorporated into the doctrines of Marxism. Early socialist writers sought to improve the conditions of the working poor. Socialism was tied to the initial efforts to form trade unions to gain workers' rights, such as a minimum wage, and to abolish dangerous labor practices, such as child labor. During the French Revolution (1788–1799), the journalist François-Noël Babeuf, commonly known as Gracchus Babeuf (1760–1797), became known for his efforts to abolish private property and the class system in France. Babeuf was executed for his radical thoughts. Many now consider Babeuf to be the first communist.

In the mid–1800s, Marx and Engels began to incorporate the main points of socialism into their new theory of Marxism. In 1841, the Communist Propaganda Society was formed in London and other communist groups began to emerge across Europe, including the Communist League, formed by Marx and Engels in 1847. In 1848, there were a series of revolutions against the existing monarchies throughout Europe. The rebellions were unsuccessful, but many governments perceived communism as one of the main motivating factors for the rebels. Therefore, communist activists were arrested, or, as in the case of Marx and others, exiled. For the remainder of the nineteenth century, communism was associated with a range of antigovernment movements in Europe and the United States. Global groups such as the First International (1864–1876) and later the Second International (1889–1916) helped spread the ideals of socialism and communism. By 1912, the Second International counted nine million members worldwide.

THE SOVIET UNION

During World War I, Russia suffered a series of humiliating defeats. By 1917, the war was very unpopular among Russians. Lenin took

Robert Owen's Utopianism

In an address on January 1, 1816, Owen described his views that people were the products of their environment and that human behavior could be changed by altering surroundings. In this passage, Owen outlines his experience at New Lanark:

I have stated that I found the population of this place similar to that of other manufacturing districts. It was, with some exceptions, existing in poverty, crime, and misery; and strongly prejudiced, as most people are at first, against any change that might be proposed. The usual mode of proceeding on the principles which have hitherto governed the conduct of men, would have been to punish those who committed the crimes, and to be highly displeased with every one who opposed the alterations that were intended for his benefit. The principles, however, upon which the new system is founded, lead to a very different conduct. They make it evident, that when men are in poverty,—when they commit crimes or actions injurious to themselves and others,—and when they are in a state of wretchedness,—there must be substantial causes for these lamentable effects; and that, instead of punishing or being angry with our fellow-men because they have been subjected to such a miserable existence, we ought to pity and commiserate them, and patiently to trace the causes whence the evils proceed, and endeavor to discover whether they may not be removed.

The First Soviet Constitution (1918)

The first Soviet Constitution formally introduced the main components of communism into law. The First Section contained the main measures to abolish the free market:

A. In order to establish the "socialization" of land, private ownership of land is abolished; all land is declared national property, and is handed over to the laboring masses, without compensation, on the basis of an equitable division giving the right of use only.

B. All forests, underground mineral wealth, and waters of national importance, all livestock and appurtenances, together with all model-farms and agricultural enterprises, are proclaimed public property.

C. As the first step toward the complete transfer of factories, works, shops, mines, railways, and other means of production and of transport to the ownership of the workers' and peasants' Soviet Republic, and in order to insure the supremacy of the laboring masses over the exploiters, the Congress ratifies the soviet law on workers' control of industry.

D. The Congress ratifies the transfer of all banks to the ownership of the workers' and peasants' government as one of the conditions insuring the emancipation of the toiling masses from the capitalistic yoke.

E. In order to exterminate all parasitic strata of society and to organize the economic life of the country, general compulsory labor is introduced.

advantage of this discontent to lead a revolution against the existing regime. Lenin's followers, the Bolsheviks, were able to seize power in what became known as the October Revolution. The Bolsheviks won the support of some Russians by promising to end participation in the unpopular war and by using the slogan "Bread and Land" as a pledge to provide food to the poor and redistribute land to the peasants. However, it was only through the use of force that they were able to maintain power. Lenin initiated the process of implementing a communist regime as Russia went through several years of civil war. Lenin withdrew Russia from World War I and moved the capital of the country from St. Petersburg to Moscow. The name of the country was changed from Russia to the Russian Soviet Federated Republic in 1918 and the Union of Soviet Socialist Republics (most often called the Soviet Union) in 1922.

Once in power, Lenin began to expropriate property and businesses from the wealthy and middle class. Major businesses, ranging from banks to factories to railroad companies, were taken over by the government. Concurrently, the regime began to seize farms and property in the countryside. All Russians were forced to work for the government in whatever occupations were needed. The Communist Party was named the official party of the Soviet Union and all other political parties were banned. In addition, a secret police force called the *Checka* was created to pursue enemies of the regime. The secret police arrested tens of thousands of prominent Russians, including teachers, businesspeople, and former government and military officials. Thousands were executed. The government also seized farms and crops. The resulting shock to the economy led to a massive famine and widespread dislocation of the population. Millions eventually died of starvation and disease. Lenin endeavored to spread communism outside of the Soviet Union. In 1919, he established the Third, or Communist, International (known as the Comintern) to replace the Second International and promote Soviet influence in communist movements around the world.

Meanwhile, there were also communist revolts in other countries, including Germany. These revolts and the creation of the Comintern led western governments such as the United States and Britain to supply weapons and troops to the anti-Bolshevik forces in the Soviet Union. When the Bolsheviks eventually won the civil war, the major

The transition to a communist economy in the Soviet Union left millions hungry and destitute. During the famine of the 1920s, a train loaded with starving Soviets leaves Tashkent Station.

powers continued to try to isolate the Soviet Union by refusing to trade with the country or engage in diplomacy with the Soviets.

By 1921, Lenin had consolidated all political power in the hands of the Communist Party. However, the economy remained devastated and millions were still on the brink of starvation. In response, Lenin developed a compromise approach, the New Economic Policy (NEP), which would have allowed free-market reforms. Many of the aspects of the NEP were similar to the later reforms undertaken by China. It seems likely that Lenin would have been willing to allow further reforms, but he suffered a stroke in 1922 and died in 1924.

Stalinism and the Cold War
After Lenin's stroke, Stalin gained greater control over the government. By the time Lenin died, Stalin was the undisputed master of the Soviet Union. Stalin consolidated his power by murdering or secretly discrediting his rivals so that there was no one who could challenge his authority. Stalin proceeded to dismantle the NEP and eliminate his opposition. He ordered a series of purges from the late 1920s through the 1930s that resulted in the deaths of as many as a million Soviet citizens (some ten million were arrested). Opponents of the regime were often sent to labor camps (known as gulags) in remote areas such as Siberia. The survival rates in the gulags were very low. Stalin also embarked on a forced collectivization project that abolished the remaining private farms in the Soviet Union. This created a new wave of famine and some five to six million Soviets died. Stalin also initiated a series of five-year plans to industrialize the Soviet Union. His brutal methods increased the number of factories and the industrial output. In addition, there were improvements in health care and education, and electricity and plumbing became widespread. However, a very large percentage of the Soviet economy was devoted to the military, which limited spending on social programs and consumer products.

During his tenure, Stalin developed a cult of personality in which people were encouraged to revere their leader in a way usually only reserved for religious figures. All accomplishments and positive steps in the country were credited to Stalin, while any problems were blamed on lesser officials. Later communist leaders would also adopt this tactic as a way of enhancing their popularity and power.

Stalin offered some support for communist groups in other

countries, but also showed that he was willing to work with anticommunist regimes to achieve his goals. In 1939, he formed a secret pact with Adolf Hitler (1889–1945) of Germany to divide Poland between the two totalitarian regimes. In June 1941, Hitler turned against Stalin and invaded the Soviet Union. During the 1930s, Stalin had purged the Soviet military and the Army was not prepared for the German invasion. Military and intelligence errors (Stalin often did not trust his own intelligence services) led to a series of devastating Soviet defeats and by December 1941, the Germans were within twenty miles of Moscow. The invasion brought the Soviets into an alliance with the Western powers, the United States, and Great Britain. To increase trust with the new allies, the Comintern was abolished. In response, the Western allies provided the Soviets with millions of dollars in aid and military equipment. The German invasion devastated the Soviet Union and some twenty million people were killed. During the war, Stalin endeavored to increase his country's power and influence and insisted that territories in Eastern Europe that were liberated from Germany be allowed to remain under the control of the Soviet Union.

In 1945, at the end of World War II, the Soviets occupied most of Central and Eastern Europe. After the war, Stalin forced these countries to accept Soviet-backed communist regimes: Albania, Bulgaria, Czechoslovakia, East Germany, Hungary, Poland, Romania, and Yugoslavia. Three once-independent countries were annexed to become part of the Soviet Union: Estonia, Latvia, and Lithuania. The states under the control of the Soviet Union were called the Soviet bloc. Stalin also tried to install pro-Soviet regimes in other countries in Europe, such as Greece and Italy, and sent Soviet troops and covert agents into countries in the Middle East, including Iran and Turkey. Stalin's actions led the United States and its allies to engage in a broad military, economic, and political effort to prevent Soviet expansion (in the United States, the strategy was called containment). Conflict between the Soviets and the United States, dubbed the Cold War, lasted until 1991. In 1949, China became a communist country and in 1959 communists under Fidel Castro (1926–) took power in Cuba. During the Cold War there were two major wars, the Korean War (1951–1953) and the Vietnam War (fought by the French, 1945–1959, and then by the United States, 1959–1974). In addition, when the communist countries of Eastern Europe tried to reform or adopt Western economic

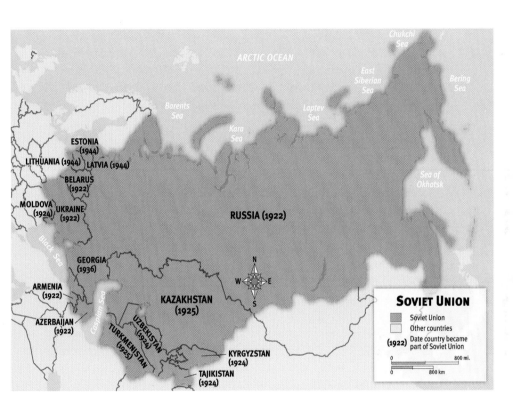

The Soviet Union

policies, they were ruthlessly suppressed by the Soviets. For instance, the Soviets led invasions of Hungary in 1956 and Czechoslovakia in 1968 in order to remove reformist regimes. Throughout the Cold War, Soviet control remained unpopular among the people of the Soviet bloc countries. To retain their influence, the Soviets stationed large numbers of troops in the region.

When Stalin died in 1953, he did not have a designated successor. The question of who would become premier led to a period of internal fighting among the senior Soviet leaders. The problem of succession was one faced by all communist regimes. In democratic countries, there is a clear chain of succession. For instance, in the United States, a president who dies in office is replaced by the vice president. Most communist governments lacked this clear succession. Some communist leaders have attempted to fix this flaw by designating a successor. However, rivals can challenge the legitimacy of the designated successor. Succession was a problem throughout the Cold War and remains an issue for contemporary communist governments.

Nikita Sergeyevitch Khrushchev (1894–1971) became leader of the Soviet Union in 1956. (He was first secretary of the Communist Party of the Soviet Union from 1953 to 1964 and chairman of the Council of Ministers from 1958 to 1964.) Khrushchev reversed many of the harshest components of Stalin's rule. He pardoned millions of people who were in the gulags and allowed discussions and exchanges about Stalin's crimes. Nonetheless, the secret police (now known as the KGB) remained and criticism of the regime was tolerated only to a limited extent. Khrushchev's reforms were cut short following the 1962 Cuban Missile Crisis when the Soviets attempted to deploy nuclear weapons in Cuba, but were forced to withdraw the weapons after their discovery by the United States. Many senior Soviet leaders believed Khrushchev had bowed to American pressure during the incident. In 1964, Khrushchev was forced from office and replaced by Leonid Brezhnev, who ruled from 1964 to 1982.

Under Brezhnev, the Soviet Union continued to support communist insurgencies around the globe. The Soviets provided military and economic support for the communist government of North Vietnam in its conflict with the United States. In addition, in 1979, the Soviet Union invaded Afghanistan to install a communist, pro-Soviet regime. The Soviet Union faced increased military and economic competition

There were a series of revolts against Soviet rule in Eastern Europe, including one in Hungary. In this 1956 photograph, Hungarian troops walk past the bodies of Soviet secret police killed during the uprising.

from the United States during the 1980s. By this period, it became clear that the Soviet economy could not keep up with the free-market economies of the United States and Western Europe. There were severe shortages of food and consumer goods. After Brezhnev's death in 1982, the Soviet Union was further weakened by a succession of older, infirm leaders, who were unable to adapt to the changing world.

In 1985, Mikhail Gorbachev, who was then only fifty-four years old, became the Soviet leader. Gorbachev endeavored to introduce market reforms to make the Soviet economy more competitive. His domestic reforms were known by the Russian word *perestroika* (reconstruction) and centered around the repeal of laws against private ownership of businesses. Gorbachev also ordered the dismantling of large state industries into smaller, more competitive units. There were also new laws to allow greater freedom of speech and of the press. In foreign policy, Gorbachev negotiated a series of arms control agreements with U.S. President Ronald Reagan (president from 1981 to 1989) that helped reduce global tensions and the need for large military expenditures. Gorbachev also ordered Soviet troops to withdraw from Afghanistan.

In 1991, hardline communists tried to overthrow Gorbachev because of their opposition to his reform efforts. The majority of people did not support the coup attempt and it was quickly suppressed. However, the incident prompted renewed independence movements in Eastern Europe and revealed that the Soviet people had lost faith in communism. By the end of the year, the Soviet Union had collapsed and the former Soviet bloc countries declared independence. In Russia, the Communist Party was banned because of the role of its leaders in the insurrection. This marked the end of the Cold War. The former Soviet bloc countries also quickly rejected communism and legalized other political parties.

CHINA

The Chinese Communist Party was formed in 1921 and its early leaders hoped to follow the example of the Bolsheviks and establish a communist regime. The Chinese communists fought against other factions in a long civil war and the party was banned by the government. Mao helped resuscitate the party in the 1920s. Mao became the leader of the communists after he helped create the party's armed wing, the Red Army, in 1927. Mao convinced other communists of the need to base their revolution on the peasantry, not urban workers. In the late 1920s

The last gasp of communism in the Soviet Union was the abortive coup in 1991. Massive crowds rallied to support Mikhail Gorbachev and his democratic reforms.

Mao's Little Red Book

The book *Quotations from Chairman Mao Zedong* was a compilation of the Chinese leader's sayings and thoughts, and excerpts from his speeches. Many of the quotations were designed to be slogans that could be easily remembered and incorporated into political teachings and indoctrination. The following line emphasizes the importance of the Communist Party: "Without the efforts of the Chinese Communist Party, without the Chinese communists as the mainstay of the Chinese people, China can never achieve independence and liberation, or industrialization and the modernization of her agriculture."

and early 1930s, the ruling government of China almost destroyed the communists. In 1934, government forces surrounded the last major communist outpost. Mao led the remaining 80,000 communists on a yearlong, 6,000-mile retreat through the mountains to escape the government forces. The trek became known as the "Long March." Only about 8,000 remained by the end of the journey. This group formed a hardcore band that was the nucleus of a new Red Army. Through the rest of the 1930s, the communists gained strength. When Japan invaded China in 1937, the government and communists suspended fighting to combat the Japanese. During World War II, the United States supplied weapons and support to the Chinese communists in their battles with the Japanese.

After World War II, a new civil war broke out between the increasingly unpopular government and the communists. Mao's forces quickly gained the upper hand. By 1949, the Red Army had conquered China. The remaining government forces fled to the island of Taiwan. In October 1949, Mao declared a communist state and renamed the country the People's Republic of China. Mao negotiated a friendship treaty with the Soviet Union, but initially concentrated on securing his control over China. As had been the case in the Soviet Union, the communists in China undertook a broad purge to arrest or execute people who could pose a threat to the regime. Intellectuals, merchants, and religious leaders fell victim to the regime. In addition, the government took control of businesses and farms, abolished private property, and began a policy of forced industrialization and collectivization of farms.

China was initially closely allied with the Soviet Union. Both countries cooperated during the Korean War. Mao also received significant foreign aid from the Soviet Union to finance industrialization. Like Stalin, Mao developed a cult of personality. After Stalin's death, Mao began to distance himself from Stalin's successors and to pursue an independent foreign policy. He also concentrated more on internal matters in China. In 1958, a new economic plan, the "Great Leap Forward," was launched. The goal was to dramatically increase industrial and food production. However, the plan failed because the goals were too ambitious and the country lacked the skilled workers to achieve the planned level of industrialization. Efforts to improve crop production by combining small and medium-sized collective farms led to a famine that killed three million people.

The Soviet Union's Vietnam

In 1979, the Soviet Union invaded Afghanistan in order to install a pro-Moscow regime. However, the Soviets quickly became bogged down in an extensive guerrilla conflict. The United States provided military equipment and training to the Islamic rebels, known as Mujahadeen. During the ten years the Soviets occupied the country, 13,833 were recorded killed (some estimates put the figure as high as 50,000) and 454,464 wounded, injured, or sick. They also lost 118 airplanes, 333 helicopters, and 147 tanks. The war cost the Soviets approximately $8 billion for each year of occupation. The cost in lives, equipment, and money made the conflict very unpopular in the Soviet Union and led many to title the conflict the Soviet Union's "Vietnam." The war in Afghanistan was one of the factors that led to the demise of the Soviet Union.

Mao wrongly suspected that antigovernment groups and rivals within the Communist Party had deliberately sabotaged the Great Leap Forward. In 1966, in an effort to purge the country of political opponents, he initiated the Cultural Revolution. Millions were arrested or killed. By 1969, Mao allowed moderate leaders back into power and the worst excesses of the Cultural Revolution ended. In the 1970s, China even began to open to the West. In 1972, U.S. President Richard M. Nixon (president, 1969–1974) visited China and opened trade relations between the two former rival nations. Mao died in 1976, and his successor, Deng Xiaoping, embarked on a broad series of economic reforms.

Market Reforms and Political Repression
Under Deng, China began to trade with other countries, including the United States. In addition, in the 1980s, the regime allowed farmers to lease plots of land and eliminated the large communes. The farmers were allowed to sell their produce and keep the profits. Deng also privatized businesses and services in cities and towns. Large factories were turned over to private firms or joint ventures between local governments and private investors. The government also established special economic zones to allow foreign companies to invest in China. As a result, while the Soviet economy stagnated in the 1980s, China's grew dramatically. Many communist leaders opposed Deng's reforms, but they allowed the economy to grow at a pace of more than 10 percent on average during the 1980s. By contrast, the Japanese economy grew at about 5 percent, while the U.S. economy grew at 3 percent during the same period.

Deng did not allow significant political reforms. In 1989, proponents of democracy staged mass protests around China. The largest of these rallies occurred in Tiananmen Square in Beijing. The regime responded by declaring martial law and killing hundreds of protestors and arresting thousands of others. The economic reforms and the crackdown at Tiananmen Square demonstrated that China had essentially ceased to be a country governed according to the principles of Marxism or Maoism. Instead, it had simply reverted to a totalitarian political regime that allowed some free-market activities.

COMMUNISM IN THE DEVELOPING WORLD
Before and during the Cold War, the United States and its allies tried to prevent the Soviet bloc from spreading communism to other

After Cuba became a communist country, Fidel Castro turned to the Soviet Union for aid and support. In 1960, Castro and Soviet leader Nikita Khrushchev met at the United Nations.

countries. However, a few countries in the developing world did become communist regimes with either Soviet or Chinese support. In the 1920s, the Soviets installed a pro-Moscow communist regime in Mongolia. In 1979, the Soviets invaded Afghanistan but withdrew after a decade of guerrilla warfare. After World War II, the Soviet Union was given control over the northern half of the Korean peninsula and Stalin established a communist regime there under Kim Il-sung in 1948. Kim ruled North Korea through a "cult of personality" dictatorship, as did his son, Kim Jong-il, after Kim Il-sung's death in 1994.

After the French withdrew from their colonies in Indochina in the 1950s, the United States became involved in a struggle to prevent the former colonies from becoming communist. The withdrawal of American forces from South Vietnam in 1974 allowed North Vietnam to unite the north and south as a single state under communist rule. Vietnam followed the Soviet model of communism and was heavily supported by Soviet economic and military aid. With support from Vietnam and the Soviet Union, communists took control of Laos in 1975. Also in 1975, a radical communist group, the Khmer Rouge, took control of Cambodia. The regime brutally forced urban dwellers into the countryside to serve as agricultural workers. Some 1.7 million Cambodians were killed, some in places that became known as the "Killing Fields."

In 1959, Cuba became a communist state. It was supported economically and militarily by the Soviet Union, but Castro incorporated elements of both Marxism-Leninism and Maoism into the Cuban government. He seized property and collectivized agriculture in an effort to develop a classless society. Castro also banned other political parties and opponents of the regime. By 1968, Castro had ushered in Soviet-style economic policies, but beginning in 1976, he allowed some economic reforms, including greater autonomy for businesses and merchants. Cuba was largely dependent on Soviet aid. When the Cold War ended and Russia ceased to provide aid, the Cuban economy declined by one-third and the country became one of the poorest in the Western Hemisphere. Castro subsequently allowed further economic reforms, but always remained ambivalent about them. There were communist insurgencies in several other Latin American states, but Nicaragua had the only other successful revolution. The Nicaraguan communists, known as the "Sandinistas," never fully implemented a Marxist-Leninist economic system. The

Sandinistas did take control of the banks and major industries and did redistribute land, but the regime allowed some private economic activities and even some opposition political parties to exist. Grenada was briefly ruled by a communist government until U.S. military intervention in 1983.

In 1970, communists took control of South Yemen, but the country was reunited with North Yemen as a noncommunist state in 1990. Several African states installed communist, or Marxist-Leninist regimes, including Benin (1975–1989), the Republic of the Congo (1964–1992), Ethiopia (1974–1991), Angola (1975–1992), and Mozambique (1975–1990).

Communism in Practice

IN THEORY, COMMUNISM IS COMPATIBLE with democracy. Most communist governments regularly held elections and claimed they were democratic. In his conception of the final communist state, Marx believed that the people would exercise control over the government. In his ideal communist state, not only would economic resources be shared, but the power of the institutions of government would be divided among the people. However, in practice, all communist regimes have proved antithetical to democracy. Instead of sharing political power, communist governments concentrate power in the hands of either a single individual or a small group. Contemporary communist regimes that allowed free elections saw the communist governments voted out of power. Among the surviving communist states, there has been some economic liberalization, as in the case of China, but few political reforms. One of the greatest problems for communist governments, and the reason for the failure of so many of the regimes, has been the trend toward totalitarianism.

THE DISTRIBUTION OF POWER IN COMMUNIST SYSTEMS

Marx believed in democracy. He argued that communism could only be achieved with the mass mobilization of the people and through their participation in the struggle to overthrow the bourgeoisie. Marx asserted that workers should be organized through local direct

Lenin and the Dictatorship of the Proletariat

Lenin viewed the period of the dictatorship of the proletariat as a time in which political and economic freedom had to be constrained in order to build the basis for later freedoms. He argued that these restrictions needed to be applied to the former ruling classes, although, in practice, the loss of freedom affected all citizens. Lenin wrote:

> The dictatorship of the proletariat, i.e., the organization of the vanguard of the oppressed as the ruling class for the purpose of suppressing the oppressors, cannot result merely in an expansion of democracy. Simultaneously with an immense expansion of democracy, which for the first time becomes democracy for the poor, democracy for the people, and not democracy for the money-bags, the dictatorship of the proletariat imposes a series of restrictions on the freedom of the oppressors, the exploiters, the capitalists. We must suppress them in order to free humanity from wage slavery, their resistance must be crushed by force; it is clear that there is no freedom and no democracy where there is suppression and where there is violence.

ЮД ЗНАМЕНЕМ ЛЕНИНА—ВПЕРЕД ЗА РОДИНУ, ЗА НАШУ ПОБЕДУ!

democracies in which all workers voted on all issues. He once said that "democracy is the road to socialism," meaning that his theoretical classless state could only be achieved once people became politically empowered. Once a classless state was achieved, democracy was necessary to ensure its continuation and retain the support of the people. In 1871, workers briefly took over the government of Paris at the end of the Franco-Prussian War, before being brutally suppressed by the French Army. Marx incorporated many of the measures of that Paris Commune into his notion of the ideal state, including: 1) replacing the standing military with an elected militia; 2) using the recall vote to replace unpopular or ineffective politicians; and also 3) using referendums to allow all citizens to decide important issues.

However, Marx believed that the democratic systems that existed during his day in countries such as Great Britain or the United States were designed to reinforce the power of the elites, not to share political power among the people. Therefore, he rejected the idea that communists could come to power through elections or the existing democratic process. This created the need for class struggle to overthrow the existing political and economic order.

Dictatorship of the Proletariat

In order for the proletariat to defeat the bourgeoisie, Marx argued that there would be a period in which the working class took control of society and implemented the necessary political and economic changes to achieve the ideal society. Workers would have to seize control of property and commerce and dismantle the existing political institutions. This period was known as the dictatorship of the proletariat and referred to control of a country by a class, the proletariat, rather than by a single individual. Marx wrote that the dictatorship of the proletariat was necessary to replace the dictatorship of the bourgeoisie (the economic elites).

Lenin used the idea of the dictatorship of the proletariat to justify the control of Russia by a small group led by a single individual. Lenin rejected Marx's ideas of direct democracy among workers' groups and instead thought political power should be concentrated in the hands of an oligarchy that would lead the people through the transition to communism. Otherwise, Lenin argued, it would be too easy for the bourgeoisie to regain power. Even after the communists took power, the bourgeoisie still had considerable power and influence and would fight the Marxist reforms. An example of this was the Russian Civil War

(1919–1922). Based on his experiences, Lenin was convinced that a period of political repression and dictatorship was necessary to dismantle all components of the old regime and implement communist ideology.

In another departure from Marx's thoughts, Lenin developed a personal dictatorship, not one based on the working class. Lenin was the undisputed leader of the Bolsheviks and when they took over he ruled the Soviet Union in much the same way as the tsars had reigned in earlier periods. He surrounded himself with a group of senior advisors (the politburo), but he reserved all decision-making authority for himself. Lenin's power was based on his twin roles as leader of the Communist Party of the Soviet Union and as the chief executive of the Soviet government. Later, Stalin grabbed even more personal power during his tenure as leader of the Soviet Union.

All communist regimes subsequently followed Lenin's model. After the communists took control of governments, they did not attempt to expand democracy. Instead, they limited power and decision making to the communist leadership. These oligarchies became increasingly based on personal loyalty and service to the leader, as opposed to merit or ability. This was especially true in regimes that developed a cult of personality around an individual figure such as Stalin or Mao.

All of the world's communist regimes developed into unitary systems in which the central government held all or most of the power and authority. Communist states used unitary systems in order to make sure that regional governments or leaders could not challenge the authority of the central bodies. Unitary governments were widespread among smaller communist states, such as Cuba or North Korea, where there was less need for multiple levels of government. However, unitary governments were also common even in large countries such as the Soviet Union and China, where there were numerous local and regional sub-governments. For instance, in the Soviet Union there were fifteen separate republics and numerous smaller governments, including autonomous regions and independent districts. The regional governments had their own legislatures and politburos, but the central government in Moscow had the power to approve or disapprove all laws, policies, and political appointments. The politburo in Moscow acted as a coordinating body to ensure uniformity among the policies and laws of the regional governments. The Soviet Constitution did give each republic the right to secede, a power not utilized until the breakup of the Soviet Union in 1991.

The Chinese State Council

In China, the equivalent of the politburo is the state council. Its members serve a fixed, five-year term, but may be, and usually are, reappointed. In Article 88, the Chinese Constitution notes that the premier "directs the work" of the council, and the nation's basic law lists the major duties and powers of the council. Article 89 contains the more important powers of the state council:

(1) To adopt administrative measures, enact administrative rules and regulations and issue decisions and orders in accordance with the Constitution and the statutes; (2) To submit proposals to the National People's Congress or its Standing Committee; (3) To lay down the tasks and responsibilities of the ministries and commissions of the State Council, to exercise unified leadership over the work of the ministries and commissions and to direct all other administrative work of a national character that does not fall within the jurisdiction of the ministries and commissions; (4) To exercise unified leadership over the work of local organs of state administration at different levels throughout the country, and to lay down the detailed division of functions and powers between the Central Government and the organs of state administration of provinces, autonomous regions and municipalities directly under the Central Government; (5) To draw up and implement the plan for national economic and social development and the state budget; (6) To direct and administer economic work and urban and rural development; (7) To direct and administer the work concerning education, science, culture, public health, physical culture and family planning; (8) To direct and administer the work concerning civil affairs, public security, judicial administration, supervision and other related matters; (9) To conduct foreign affairs and conclude treaties and agreements with foreign states; (10) To direct and administer the building of national defense; (11) To direct and administer affairs concerning the nationalities and to safeguard the equal rights of minority nationalities and the right of autonomy of the national autonomous areas

The Communist Party

All of the world's communist parties were (and are still) structured in a similar fashion. Party members were organized into local groups or cells. Each group was originally known in Russia as a *soviet* (Russian for "council"), the term that produced the name of the Soviet Union. The soviets had a quasi-governmental role in replacing local authorities and governments. Ideally, the soviets engaged in direct democracy and made joint decisions. By the 1920s, the soviets were firmly under the control of the central government.

Representatives from each local party organization were elected to national conventions known as party congresses. These congresses were held every several years or during national emergencies. The congresses were supposed to decide grand matters of policy through open debate and voting. In addition, the congresses elected a central committee to run the government in between meetings of the congress. The central committee chose the national executive (the politburo) from its members. The politburo functioned like a cabinet and oversaw the daily operations of the government and military. Members were appointed to lead specific ministries or departments. Hence, politburo members were given positions such as minister of defense or minister of trade, similar to those in noncommunist governments. The politburo elected a leader known as either the secretary-general or simply as the chairman.

The system was designed so that power and authority flowed from the local soviets up to the politburo and secretary-general. However, in reality, decisions were made by the politburo, which imposed its will on the other components of the government and party. Also, instead of the central committee choosing the politburo, the reverse was true. The politburo appointed members to the central committee, which in turn controlled the party congresses. These meetings soon lost real importance and simply became vehicles through which the politburo could rally support for programs or policies or explain actions.

The post of secretary-general became a lifetime appointment and was combined with the political title of premier. This allowed communist leaders to be the formal head of both the party and the government. From Lenin onward, the office of premier became dictatorial. This was especially true in those regimes that developed a cult of personality around their

e Supreme Soviet

ctions and organization of the Supreme Soviet were detailed
936 Constitution of the Soviet Union. The Constitution gives
idium of the Supreme Soviet wide powers, most of which are
in Article 49 of the basic law:

he Presidium of the Supreme Soviet of the U.S.S.R.:
Convenes the sessions of the Supreme Soviet of the
U.S.S.R.;

nterprets laws of the U.S.S.R. in operation, issues
decrees;

Dissolves the Supreme Soviet of the U.S.S.R. in
conformity with Article 47 of the Constitution of the
U.S.S.R. and orders new elections;

Conducts referendums on its own initiative or on the
demand of one of the Union Republics;

Annuls decisions and orders of the Council of People's
Commissars of the U.S.S.R. and of the Councils of
People's Commissars of the Union Republics in case
they do not conform to law;

n the intervals between sessions of the Supreme Soviet
of the U.S.S.R., relieves of their posts and appoints
People's Commissars of the U.S.S.R. on the recom-
mendation of the Chairman of the Council of People's
Commissars of the U.S.S.R., subject to subsequent con-
firmation by the Supreme Soviet of the U.S.S.R.;

ards decorations and confers titles of honor of the

Exercises the right of pardon;

Appoints and removes the higher commands of the armed forces of the U.S.S.R.;

In the intervals between sessions of the Supreme Soviet of the U.S.S.R., proclaims a state of war in the event of armed attack on the U.S.S.R., or whenever necessary to fulfill international treaty obligations concerning mutual defense against aggression;

Orders general or partial mobilization;

Ratifies international treaties;

Appoints and recalls plenipotentiary representatives of the U.S.S.R. to foreign states;

Receives the credentials and letters of recall of diplomatic representatives accredited to it by foreign states;

Proclaims martial law in separate localities or throughout the U.S.S.R. in the interests of the defense of the U.S.S.R. or for the purpose of ensuring public order and state security.

ruler. Once a new chairman was selected, the politburo had only marginal influence over policy decisions. Only once, in the case of Khrushchev, was a secretary-general removed from office by the politburo. Almost all other communist leaders throughout the world served until they died or until communism was overthrown in their country.

The Communist Party in Marxist regimes was supposed to exemplify ideals of a classless society. However, in most states, the Party represented a social and economic class that had the same degree of power and wealth as the former bourgeoisie. Membership in the Communist Party was usually limited to about 10 percent of the population and members were either recommended by current members or carefully scrutinized before they were admitted to the Party.

Party members in communist regimes often enjoyed special privileges and rights. Government and senior military positions were reserved for party members. Membership in the party in several countries also gave people access to special stores that contained products and goods unavailable to the general public. Membership sometimes meant better housing. For instance, in the Soviet Union, just prior to the end of the communist government, 40 percent of the population survived on 200 rubles per month, while 78 percent of the population lived on 285 or fewer rubles per month. Most leaders of the Communist Party earned about 1,030 rubles per month, and the top party leaders were paid 2,850 rubles. Party leaders were able to acquire Western-made goods, such as Mercedes-Benz automobiles and electronic equipment, and even own vacation homes. While the party elites constituted a wealthy upper class, party membership often offered only marginal benefits for most.

In the Soviet Union, the elite party members were known as the *nomenklatura* (Russian for "the list," initially a list of top government and military positions). The nomenklatura included members of the politburo and their staffs, members of the central committee, senior military officers, members of the supreme court, union leaders, directors of industries, heads of scientific institutes, university leaders, and regional and local leaders. These positions were supposed to be based on merit, but in practice they came to be awarded based on a combination of loyalty and personal connections. Nomenklatura typically held their posts for life. By the 1970s, more than half of all nomenklatura in the Soviet bloc states had held their posts for more than fifteen years. The nomenklatura in the Soviet Union numbered about 750,000 people in a country with a population of more than 300 million. During the same time period, in Poland, the nomenklatura numbered about 13,000 out of a population of 35 million, and 2,252 in tiny Estonia with a population of 1.1 million.

LEGISLATURES

Communist countries have different names for their legislatures, but these bodies have similar features. One key characteristic of all communist legislatures is their lack of power. Whether examining past governments, such as the Soviet Union, or contemporary regimes, such as China, legislatures mainly act to rubber-stamp the decisions or policies of that country's politburo.

In the Soviet Union, the legislature was the Supreme Soviet. It had two chambers: the Soviet of the Union and the Soviet of Nationalities. Each chamber was equal in power and could initiate legislation. The Soviet of the Union had one deputy for every 300,000 people (by 1989, it had 750 deputies). Representation in the Soviet of Nationalities was divided among the regional governments of the Soviet Union. Each republic, such as Ukraine or Russia, had thirty-two deputies, while other regions had between one and eleven deputies (in 1989, there were also 750 representatives in the Soviet of Nationalities). The Supreme Soviet was the only body that could pass constitutional amendments, and it appointed the supreme court and elected the presidium (an executive council of legislative bodies of the Soviet Union). In practice, the Supreme Soviet was not a real deliberative body and it simply formalized measures favored by the politburo. Power was exercised through the presidium, which held most executive functions. Members of the presidium served only with the tacit approval of the politburo. The Supreme Soviet had two sessions per year, but was adjourned during party congresses. While its members were elected for four-year terms, the elections had little meaning. Local soviets chose the candidates and ensured that only one person ran for each position. Thus, there were elections, but people could only vote for one candidate. Each of the regional governments in the Soviet Union had a regional supreme soviet that had a single chamber. Those states in Eastern Europe that were in the Soviet bloc had similar legislative bodies.

In China, the highest legislative body is the National People's

Congress (NPC). The NPC has 3,000 deputies. It only meets for two weeks each year, concurrently with the national meeting of the Chinese Communist Party. Delegates to the NPC are elected by local Communist Party organizations. When the NPC is not in session, legislative matters are handled by the 150-member standing committee of the NPC. Neither the NPC nor the standing committee has any real political power and, instead, the legislature rubber-stamps measures proposed by the Chinese politburo. The NPC officially elects China's leader, but the body has always chosen the candidate preferred by the ruling oligarchy.

North Korea has a legislature that is very similar to the NPC. The Supreme Deputies Assembly (SDA) consists of 687 deputies who are elected for five-year terms (as in the Soviet Union, there is only one political party and therefore a single candidate selected for each office). The SDA is rarely in session and legislative matters are usually overseen by a committee, the presidium, which is elected from the membership of the legislature. All real political power is concentrated in the hands of North Korea's dictator.

Cuba's legislature is also modeled on the NPC. It is known as the National Assembly of People's Power. The body has 609 deputies who are elected for five-year terms. The candidates are nominated in local meetings, but they have to be approved by the government. Officially anyone can run for office, but all representatives are members of the ruling Communist Party. The legislature only meets briefly twice a year and it does not initiate legislation. Instead it simply approves measures or policies put forth by the government.

In Laos, the legislature is called the National Assembly and consists of 109 representatives. The representatives are elected for five-year terms. The National Assembly follows the model of other communist legislatures, although in 2002, a nonparty candidate was allowed to run for and won a seat in the Assembly.

In Vietnam, the legislature is also known as the National Assembly. It has 498 members who are elected for five-year terms. The Vietnamese asssembly elects the country's president. In the 2002 elections, fifty-four representatives were elected who were not affiliated with Vietnam's ruling Communist Party.

4
Political and Economic Development ▪ ▪ ▪

CENTRAL TO COMMUNISM is the concept of political and economic equality. Marx envisioned the system as the best way to ensure that all people had the same degree of freedom and power, and an equal standard of living. Leaders of the communist revolutions in Russia, China, and Cuba asserted that they sought to overthrow the class systems in their countries and create egalitarian societies. But communist systems were totalitarian and antidemocratic. While the regimes often did improve the lives of the poorest people, they did so partly by lowering the standard of living of a country's other social and economic groups. In addition, instead of eliminating ethnic, racial, religious, or gender discrimination, communist regimes often brutally suppressed groups that were outside of the mainstream, such as Gypsies, homosexuals, or religious minorities. Finally, over time, elites such as the nomenklatura came to dominate the political and economic orders, creating a new class structure that was often even more rigid than the regime it replaced.

COLLECTIVISM AND TOTALITARIANISM

The French philosopher Jean-Jacques Rousseau wrote that government should exist for the common good. In other words, government should do the most good for the largest number of people. In democracies, governments attempt to balance Rousseau's ideas about the common good with the ideas of the British philosopher John Locke (1632–1704), who emphasized the importance of individual rights. Under communist systems, however, the common good was more important than the rights of individuals. Thus, communist governments were willing to take away from people individual rights, such as the right to own property or freedom of speech, if the regime believed it would be for the greater good of society. One common feature of communist regimes is the loss of civil liberties and civil rights. The loss of these rights and freedoms was unpopular and opposed by many in new communist states. Therefore, governments had to adopt strict and repressive measures to ensure continued communist control of the country. The number of those killed, injured, and tortured by communist governments will never be accurately known, but a 1999 study estimated the number of deaths in a range of countries: 65 million in the People's Republic of China; 20 million in the Soviet Union; 2 million in Cambodia; 2 million in North Korea; 1.7 million in the communist states of Africa; 1.5 million in Afghanistan; 1 million in Vietnam; 1 million in the communist countries of Eastern and Central Europe; 150,000 in the communist regimes of Latin America, including Cuba and Nicaragua.

Political Repression
In order to ensure that the regime could impose its policies, the communist government would limit people's ability to criticize leaders or policies. This repression took several forms. People were not allowed to publicly voice opposition to the regime or its policies. In addition, noncommunist political parties were banned. People risked arrest or detention if they objected to communism. Anyone who opposed communist ideology was judged to have "immature" or "bourgeois" beliefs. In order to overcome these incorrect beliefs, the person would undergo intense political indoctrination, known commonly as reeducation. Reeducation might involve special classes or it could mean confinement in a psychiatric institution or it could result in exile to a work camp for one to twenty years. Between 1931 and 1950 in the Soviet Union, an average of five million people were confined in work camps (the mortality rate in the camps during this period is estimated at 10 to 30 percent). In China, during Mao's reign, there was an average of 10–15 million people in work camps (with a mortality rate between 5 and 10 percent). Even members of the Communist Party were not

safe from repression. During the Cultural Revolution in China, more than one million party members were executed because they were believed to oppose Mao's ideas. After the fall of South Vietnam in 1975, several hundred thousand were killed by the victorious communists in reeducation camps.

In some cases, the communists tried to eliminate whole groups of people. This was often because specific groups were perceived as being especially strong supporters of the bourgeoisie or because they were perceived to be especially anticommunist. For instance, during World War II, Stalin exiled large numbers of ethnic minorities to work camps, including Chechens, Tatars, Ukrainians, and ethnic Germans. After communism was installed in Poland and Czechoslovakia, 11 million ethnic Germans were exiled from their homes in these countries (some 1.5 million died of hunger or disease while they tried to relocate to Western nations). In Vietnam, Montagnards, a group that allied itself with the United States during the Vietnam War, continue to face discrimination and repression. As late as 2001, a government crackdown led more than 5,000 Montagnards to flee to neighboring countries seeking asylum.

Religion is seen as one of the main threats to communism. All communist states are officially atheist, although there are varying degrees of toleration for religion. The communists want people to abandon their private religions and instead believe in communist ideology with the same passion and zeal. Communists also contend that religion is used by the bourgeoisie as a way to keep people servile and compliant, making them believe they will be rewarded in heaven for their meekness on earth. Marx said that "religion is the opiate of the masses," meaning that faith is used like a drug to dull people's awareness of their poor surroundings and low standard of living.

Consequently, all communist states, past and present, limit religious freedom. For instance, when Stalin came to power, he closed some 5,000 synagogues in the Soviet Union. From 1949 until 1965, religion and religious services were allowed in China, but following the Cultural Revolution, all religion was brutally suppressed. Priests were arrested, churches were taken over by the state, and foreign missionaries were forced to leave the country. Most churches and temples were destroyed, and most graveyards with religious symbols were converted to agricultural space. Since the 1970s, China has begun to tolerate some religious groups and services, but many faiths continue

Khrushchev Repudiates Stalin's Repression

Stalin used highly brutal methods to suppress his real or imagined enemies. His actions were so terrible that his successor, Khrushchev, rejected Stalin's policies during a secret speech on February 25, 1956, titled "On the Personality Cult and Its Consequences." In the address, Khrushchev was especially critical of the practice of the government to declare someone an "enemy of the people" and then torture the individual to confess to various crimes (whether or not the person had committed a crime). In the speech, Khrushchev declared that:

> Stalin originated the concept "enemy of the people." This term automatically made it unnecessary that the ideological errors of a man or men engaged in a controversy be proven. It made possible the use of the cruelest repression, violating all norms of revolutionary legality, against anyone who in any way disagreed with Stalin, against those who were only suspected of hostile intent, against those who had bad reputations. The concept of "enemy of the people" actually eliminated the possibility of any kind of ideological fight or the making of one's views known on this or that issue, even [matters] of a practical nature. On the whole, the only proof of guilt actually used, against all norms of current legal science, was the "confession" of the accused himself. As subsequent probing has proven, "confessions" were acquired through physical pressures against the accused. This led to glaring violations of revolutionary legality and to the fact that many entirely innocent individuals [people] who in the past had defended the Party line became victims.

Communists sought to suppress religion, which they saw as a threat to their ideology. In 1925, German communists displayed anti-religious propaganda. The slogan on the truck reads: "Religion is the opium of the people."

to be suppressed. Tibetans (who are mainly Buddhist) and Uighurs (a Muslim group) face special repression from the government because of their religious beliefs. For example, the communists forced many Tibetan monks and nuns, who had taken vows of celibacy, to marry. Other communist countries have loosened religious restrictions. In 1991, Cuba allowed religious believers to join the Communist Party for the first time. Cuba amended its constitution in 1992 to ban religious discrimination, although there continues to be interference in religious matters. For instance, the government has allowed only a handful of churches and synagogues to be built since 1990.

Police State

Communist regimes, like other totalitarian governments, remain in power by creating police states. A police state is a country in which the government derives its authority through the use of the police, spies, and military, rather than from the support of the people. Security forces in a police state seldom operate according to national law. Instead, they use brutality and the threat of extreme punishment to force the population to obey the government. Police states cannot be democratic since democracies operate according to the rule of law. For instance, in a country run by the rule of law, the police must have a reason before they can arrest someone. The police are usually seen as servants of the people who are there to "protect and serve" citizens. In a police state, the security forces often arrest or detain people for no reason. Such tactics create a culture of fear and suspicion that is designed to prevent people from opposing the regime.

Police states usually employ a special type of security force, known as the secret police or political police, to help maintain order and crush dissent. The mission of the secret police is to deal with internal threats within a communist or totalitarian regime. Officers operate in secret and often conceal their identity. Unlike the conventional police force, the secret police usually do not need a warrant or other official document to question or arrest a suspect. In addition, their interrogations and operations are secret. They often use informants who provide information on potential enemies or illicit activities. This means people in communist states have to be very suspicious and careful of their words and actions since their friends and even family members might be informants. Suspects who were detained by the secret police were often tortured in order to get them to provide names of other opponents of the regime. People often gave names of anyone in order to stop the torture. Thus, many innocent people were arrested and forced to provide more names, creating a continuous source of detentions and torture.

ECONOMIC COLLECTIVIZATION

One of the first actions taken by communists when they gain control of a government is the takeover of businesses and farms. In order to achieve a classless, Marxist society, all economic activity must be collectivized so that everyone benefits equally from any wealth or resources produced. The process of taking property and assets is

The KGB

From 1954 until 1991, the Soviet Union's secret police was the KGB (*Komitet Gosudarstvennoi Bezopasnosti*, which translates as the State Security Committee). The KGB combined the existing secret police and the Soviet intelligence agencies into one large organization. The KGB had three main functions. First, it conducted intelligence operations in foreign countries. Second, it undertook counterintelligence operations within the Soviet bloc countries to prevent Western spies from gathering information or recruiting agents. Third, the KGB suppressed opponents of the regime and maintained internal security. In 1967, the KGB prepared a report for the politburo which detailed the specifics of many of its operations. The top secret report was "KGB 1967 Annual Report," delivered to Premier Leonid Brezhnev on May 6, 1968. At the time, there were 167,000 KGB agents in the Soviet Union in a population of 220 million. In addition, about 57,000 agents were stationed overseas or involved in foreign intelligence operations. During 1967, the KGB recruited 218 foreigners to act as spies. The organization arrested and tried 34 suspected spies in the Soviet Union. One of the largest internal operations the KGB undertook that year was the confiscation of some 11,856 leaflets and flyers that were critical of the regime. Nearly 1,200 people were arrested for their part in writing, printing, or distributing the anticommunist literature. Some 730 other people were arrested for antiregime activities, including 221 who were trying to leave the Soviet Union without permission and 148 who were caught smuggling goods into the country. Furthermore, 2,293 people were questioned about anticommunist activities and 6,747 were followed, or had listening devices placed on their phones or in their homes, by the KGB. Finally, more than 12,000 people were interviewed by the KGB and warned that if they engaged in any anti-Soviet activities they would be arrested or tortured or face other sanctions.

known as nationalization. In some cases, people or companies were compensated when their property or resources were expropriated, but in most cases, communist regimes did not pay owners for their losses. Instead, the governments took control of factories, businesses, transport, and other forms of commerce.

Most communist regimes followed a model developed by Stalin. The government would develop long-term plans that identified specific targets and goals for the economy. Stalin announced his first Five-Year Plan in 1928. The program called for the mass collectivization of all farms and set nationwide industrialization as the nation's main priority. Stalin sought to increase the industrial output of the Soviet Union so that it was comparable to that of the United States or Great Britain. Within five years, Stalin wanted overall industrial output increased by 250 percent, and heavy industry expanded by 330 percent. To achieve this, people who were engaged in agriculture would be forced to move to the cities and work in factories. However, Stalin believed that food output would actually be increased, despite the loss of farmworkers, because farms would be combined into massive agricultural collectives. Some five million farmers were sent to work camps in Siberia because they resisted collectivization. The loss of experienced farmers resulted in a massive famine that killed millions more. The unrealistic industrial goals were never met, although Stalin's efforts did dramatically increase the industrial base of the Soviet Union. Industrial production increased by about 50 percent — a significant accomplishment, but at a high cost. Throughout the 1930s, industrial output expanded by an average of 16.5 percent.

There were positive results from the succession of five-year plans. Electrical production increased by 133 percent and for the first time in history, a majority of Soviets had access to electricity. Between 1928 and 1940, railroad lines expanded from 77,900 to 106,100 kilometers (or 48,300 to 65,782 miles). This expanded the flow of goods and products and led passenger traffic to increase by 400 percent. There were also dramatic expansions in health care and the government initiated the first widespread vaccination program. Later Soviet five-year plans usually had the same mixed results.

China also utilized five-year plans, with the first put in place in 1952. China had greater success as Mao's government set more modest goals and the Chinese received economic aid from the Soviet Union during the first plan (about $300 million). By 1957, the Chinese had exceeded goals in the production of key resources such as coal, iron, steel, oil, cement, and chemical fertilizer. China continues to use five-year plans (the tenth such program was put in place in 2001), but the goals have shifted dramatically away from industrialization. In the tenth plan, the priority is to invest some $87.7 billion to improve the environment. The eleventh plan, announced in 2005, sets a goal of improving social and economic equality. Vietnam also continues to utilize five-year plans. Its 2001 to 2005 plan calls for a shift toward free-market enterprises and away from state-owned industries and to integrate into the global economy to a greater extent.

Centralized Planning
To formulate a five-year plan, communist states follow similar patterns. The politburo or central committee sets broad goals, such as increased industrialization. These guidelines are submitted to a party congress for approval (there is usually little debate or discussion and approval is almost always automatic). The priorities are transmitted from the congress to the government or ministers who develop specific goals and policies related to their individual areas. Once a broad plan is developed by the ministers, it is passed to a body usually known as the state planning commission (SPC). The SPC is composed of professional bureaucrats who represent all sectors of the economy. The SPC then manages the day-to-day operations of the economy and sets specific short-term goals, such as monthly production quotas.

When developing five-year plans, communist countries usually divide products into two broad categories. The first is Group A goods, which include industrial products, minerals, and heavy machinery. Most governments emphasize the production of Group A products in order to increase industrialization and future economic growth. The second class of items is Group B products such as consumer goods and items for personal use. After the death of Stalin, the Soviets increased the emphasis on Group B products, but they were never able to keep up with demand. The five-year plans of the 1970s and 1980s called for the production of Group B products to increase more than 5 percent per year.

Because production goals are set over a five-year span, there is often little ability to adjust to changes in the economy or shifts in population. For instance, for Group B goods, the SPC might plan on the production of a certain number of coats, but if there is an especially

China's Tenth Five-Year Plan

In its March 2001 session, the People's Congress approved the c
tenth five-year plan. The plan bore little resemblance to earlier p
because of its emphasis on improving the environment. The pl
for broad initiatives to protect and enhance the economy. Actu
plan declared:

> We need to protect and make proper use of valuabl
> resources such as fresh water, farmland and energy ir
> accordance with the law. We must gradually establisl
> a system of reserves for strategically important minera
> resources and ensure their safe supply. We need tc
> strengthen the comprehensive development, utilizatior
> and conservation of marine resources. We need tc
> increase our recycling of resources in order to utilize
> our resources more effectively. We need to improve the
> system of paying compensation for the use of natura
> resources. We must safeguard the rights and interests o
> the state as the owner of mineral and other resources
> We must improve laws and regulations in this regard
> and strengthen law enforcement. . . . We need tc
> continue our efforts to control and treat water pollutior
> in important river valleys, regions and sea areas. We
> need to treat pollution in large and medium cities
> with the aim of noticeably improving the quality of the
> environment there. We also need to pay due attentior
> to prevention and control of environmental pollution ir
> rural areas, especially chemical pollution in agricultura
> production. We need to improve environmental
> meteorological and seismological monitoring to helf
> prevention and reduction of natural disasters.

cold winter when people want more, or thicker, coats, it is difficult to adapt and increase production. On the other hand, if the winter is very warm, there would be an overabundance of coats. Consequently, during the five-year cycles, there are large surpluses of some products and severe shortages of others. For instance, by 1988, the Soviet Union produced almost twice as much milk per person as either the United States or Great Britain. However, at the same time, of all the major consumer goods, only furniture manufacturers met their quotas. There were shortages of electronic products, appliances, clothing, and paper products. The constant consumer shortages undermined confidence in the communist regime in the Soviet Union and contributed to the fall of the government. Other communist countries adapted their economic planning to allow free-market reforms in order to provide more consumer goods.

5
Communism in Perspective

COMMUNISM DEVELOPED as a political ideology that would foster the creation of Marxist-based societies. Communist leaders and their supporters believed that their political system would erase the inequities and unfairness of modern countries. They argued that the bourgeoisie in contemporary democracies manipulated the political and economic structures so that the bourgeoisie benefited more than other groups. By eliminating the bourgeoisie, communists insisted that equality could be achieved. However, in the late 1980s and early 1990s, most communist countries abandoned Marxism and instead turned to democracy and the free market. Even the remaining communist powers of the world have taken various steps to move away from Marxism and toward the free market. The rejection of many of the main concepts of communism brings into question whether the ideology can form a viable political system.

COMMUNISM AND POLITICAL CONTROL
Most scholars agree that communism has never been implemented in the way Marx envisioned. Instead, each communist state adapted the system to conform with its particular political culture (those traditions, values, and principles that form the basis for a nation's politics). A country's economic status also affects the manner in which communism is implemented. Communism in the Soviet Union was different

from communism in China or Cuba. One problem that confronted communist countries such as the Soviet Union or China was that these nations did not have a political culture or history that included democracy. Instead these countries had a tradition of dictatorships and the communist systems that replaced the old-fashioned dictatorships were totalitarian in nature. Nonetheless, communist regimes declared that they were democratic and even held regular elections. This was done to make the government appear legitimate and representative of the people. Instead, the communist governments kept control of the electoral process and only candidates approved by the Communist Party were elected to office.

Elections
As noted, all communist regimes have involved some degree of dictatorial rule. But even though political power is concentrated in the Communist Party, elections are regularly held. For instance, in the Soviet Union the elections were officially very open and free and conducted according to the Constitution. On paper, the Soviets had an electoral system similar to Western democracies. In reality, the elections were tightly controlled and the people exercised no control over the political system. Until 1987 in the Soviet Union, local party leaders and other officials selected the communist candidate for each office. There was only one candidate, so whoever was chosen by the party would be the winner. Everyone was required by law to vote. Election officials commonly went to hospitals to make sure sick people voted. Therefore, the candidates were usually elected with 99 percent or more of the vote. (A few people who were opposed to the regime would not choose a candidate.) Unlike democracies, voting was not always done by secret ballot. Instead, local officials or the KGB monitored voting booths.

Elections did allow people some ability to influence government. It became common practice for citizens to write concerns or requests for certain services or changes in policy on their ballots. Sometimes, local governments would respond to these requests or alter policy if there was enough feedback from the public. In 1985, in one local election in the Soviet town of Krasnoyarsk, a number of people requested the construction of a civic center and the party subsequently built the facility. In another area that year, citizens asked that an airport be moved and it was. In 1987, the Soviet Union allowed multicandidate

Communist regimes claimed to be democratic. However, votes were coordinated and the outcome always predictable. Communist Party members voted by holding up a card.

elections (although everyone had to be a member of the Communist Party) in 5 percent of local elections. The first multiparty elections in the modern era did not occur until after the fall of communism in 1991.

Beginning in the 1980s, China began to allow elections for local posts. Previously, all local officials were appointed by the Communist Party. Now, elections are held for town or village committees and local executives. Currently, about 90 percent of China's villages, towns, and cities elect their local leaders. Opposition parties are still banned, but independents may run for office. Also, members of the Communist Party may campaign against each other. Candidates must still be approved by the Communist Party. By 1998, more than 65 percent of local elections involved more than one candidate. However, the elected town chief has to serve alongside a local party secretary who continues to be appointed by the central government. This limits the power of the elected officials (who also have to be careful of the secret police). In addition, political culture continues to discriminate against women. Only a small number of women hold office in China. Among the 111 towns in Zhejiang province, there is only one female village chief.

PROPAGANDA AND MEDIA CONTROL

In an effort to maintain support and stifle dissent, communist regimes maintain rigid control over the information people can obtain. From the formation of the Soviet Union onward, all communist governments have controlled the media and press and used propaganda to shape people's opinions and ideas. Communist states generally do not allow free or independent news reporting. Instead, communist states have official news agencies that print newspapers and control broadcast media. According to the World Press Freedom Ranking in 2003, all of the contemporary communist countries ranked very low in press freedom. Out of 166 spots, North Korea ranked 166; Cuba, 165; Laos, 163; China, 161; and Vietnam, 159. By contrast, Finland ranked number one and the United States tied with Greece at 31. Many former communist countries actually ranked very high. Latvia was number 11, while the Czech Republic, Slovakia, and Estonia all tied at 12.

Often in communist regimes journalists are jailed if they write or report stories that are critical of the regime. In addition, communist governments try to prevent citizens from gaining access to foreign reports or media. The Soviet Union imposed strict bans on the

Elections in the Soviet Union

The 1977 Constitution of the Soviet Union contained many duplicitous statements. On paper, the document declared that the Soviets had an election system comparable to any democracy. Citizens older than eighteen were allowed to vote, and people only had to be twenty-one years of age to hold office. In addition, elections were paid for by the state. The Constitution had the principle of one person-one vote and elections were supposed to be through secret ballot. However, Article 100 also noted that candidates were chosen by the party and affiliated organizations:

Article 96
1) Elections shall be universal: all citizens of the USSR who have reached the age of 18 shall have the right to vote and to be elected, with the exception of persons who have been certified insane. 2) To be eligible for election to the Supreme Soviet of the USSR a citizen of the USSR must have reached the age of 21.

Article 97
Elections shall be equal: each citizen shall have one vote; all voters shall exercise the franchise on an equal footing.

Article 98
Elections shall be direct: deputies to all Soviets of People's Deputies shall be elected by direct vote.

Article 99
Voting at elections shall be secret: control over voters' exercise of the franchise is inadmissible.

Article 100
1) The following shall have the right to nominate candidates: branches and organizations of the Communist Party of the Soviet Union, trade unions, and the All-Union Leninist Young Communist League; cooperatives and other public organizations; work collectives, and meetings of servicemen in their military units. 2) Citizens of the USSR and public organizations are guaranteed the right to free and all-round discussion of the political and personal qualities and competence of candidates, and the right to campaign for them at meetings, in the press, and on television and radio. 3) The expenses involved in holding elections to Soviets of People's Deputies shall be met by the state.

possession of foreign newspapers and even used electronic jamming to prevent reception of European television and radio. By the 1970s and 1980s, the Soviets were especially intent on preventing their people from seeing the superior quality of life in Western Europe. All contemporary communist states heavily censor or limit access to the Internet. In North Korea, ordinary citizens cannot access the Internet. In China, the Internet is censored and the government keeps track of people's usage. Certain keywords or phrases cannot be posted, and they trigger alarms if they are keyed. In addition, some searches are blocked. In order to have access to the Chinese economy, Internet companies such as Google have to agree to censor some of their content. Cybercafés must keep logs of use by customers for sixty days. In 2004, sixty-one people in China were arrested for illegally using the Internet.

Education and Indoctrination

Communist efforts to control opinions and beliefs begin when children are still very young. School curriculums in communist countries include significant political indoctrination. Communist educational systems emphasize rote learning and discourage independent thinking. The curriculums do not include science projects or creative essays. Instead the more students are able to memorize materials, the higher their grades. In addition, in the Soviet Union there were special schools for aspiring members of the Communist Party, and once a person joined the party, there might have been additional courses and training that lasted from one to four years. For instance, until the fall of the Soviet Union, party members from the USSR and its allies sent students to the Advanced Party School in Moscow for specialized courses in ideology and governance. In addition to formal education, the party also provided special seminars and presentations on Marxism and communism to average citizens.

Repetition is one of the keys to communist ideology. Lenin and his successors in the Soviet Union and abroad made extensive use of slogans and mottos. These slogans were designed to reinforce communism. Often people recited them as part of greetings to each other and the mottos were used in school lessons or as part of official ceremonies. Some were very simple, such as these early Soviet mottos: "Long Live Marxism-Leninism" or "Proletarians of All Nations, Unite." One series of Soviet posters showed construction workers and read "Building a Communist Paradise." Common

Most aspects of everyday life in the Soviet Union were highly regimented. In this photograph from 1961, Soviet workers perform daily exercises at a watch factory.

Our March

One of the most famous Soviet propaganda films was *Our March*, which chronicled the history of the Soviet Union from the 1917 revolution through World War II. The film was released in 1968 to mark the fiftieth anniversary of the communist takeover of Russia. Many consider the short movie a masterpiece. It combined archival footage and scenes from other Soviet propaganda movies to present a story that praises the actions of Soviet leaders and ignores their mistakes or problems. There were speeches by Lenin and news footage of the 1917 revolt and World War II. When no real footage of an event existed, the movie took scenes from older works of propaganda. Enemies of the regime, including the bourgeoisie, Nazis, or Western governments, were portrayed as villainous and cruel. Instead of showing one scene at a time, the film is presented in a widescreen format that divides the screen into three panels and shows different events linked together by a narrator. There is also a stirring soundtrack. The film is a model for other Soviet propaganda pieces. It was produced in both Russian and English so it could be shown to Western audiences.

Chinese slogans included "Serve the People" or "Achieve the Four Modernizations" (referring to the effort to modernize science, agriculture, industry, and defense). During the government effort to slow population growth in China, tens of thousands of posters were distributed reading "It is Good to Have Just One Child." Some phrases were more complicated. In Cuba, in an effort to promote community service, there were large billboards that contained a quote from Fidel Castro: "Never Neglect Voluntary Work for it is the Cornerstone of Our Communist Education." Such slogans were designed to provide simple credos for people to live by and to replace religious phrases or traditional sayings, which the communists believed reflected bourgeois sentiments and undermined the regime.

Posters and large pictures were also common in the workplace and public spaces. These portrayed heroic figures from history or showed stylized contemporaries promoting the tenets of communism. Of course, the posters usually were designed to reinforce communist slogans. Often the posters were produced in a series to tell a story. For instance, the Soviets made poster series to commemorate the 1917 revolution, the first five-year plan, and various aspects of World War II. Communist regimes also made extensive use of propaganda films. These movies glorified communism and presented distorted views of Western democracies and their social or cultural problems.

Communist countries also make extensive use of youth organizations to indoctrinate children and young adults. Children under the age of thirteen belong to the Young Pioneers. The Young Pioneers receive special political training and participate in a range of community activities, including ceremonies, parades, and volunteer work, such as repairing homes or buildings. The organization was created to take the place of groups such as the Boy Scouts or Girl Scouts. In Cuba, the organization is known as the José Martí Young Pioneers (in honor of a Cuban revolutionary hero), and numbers 1.4 million children. In Vietnam, the organization is known as the Ho Chi Minh Young Pioneer Organization (in honor of the founder of Communist Vietnam) and numbers 2.5 million members.

Youths fourteen and older join the Young Communist League or Youth League, which conducts political education, summer camps, and some military training. The organization is often used as a supplemental work force and can be mobilized during emergencies. For instance, in Cuba, following hurricanes or severe tropical storms,

Chinese Young Pioneers perform at the opening of the Fourteenth Communist Youth League Congress in Beijing on June 19, 1998.

Communist Youth League of China

The Communist Youth League is deemed so important to China that the country included information on the organization in Chapter X of its constitution. Specifically, the constitution defines the nature of the league and pledges party support for the body, allowing league officers to attend party meetings:

Article 49:
The Communist Youth League of China is a mass organization of advanced young people under the leadership of the Communist Party of China; it is a school where a large number of young people learn about socialism with Chinese characteristics and about communism through practice; it is the Party's assistant and reserve force. The Central Committee of the Communist Youth League functions under the leadership of the Central Committee of the Party. The local chapters of the Communist Youth League are under the leadership of the Party committees at the corresponding levels and of the higher organizations of the League itself.

Article 50:
Party committees at all levels must strengthen their leadership over the Communist Youth League organizations and pay attention to selecting and training League cadres. The Party must firmly support the Communist Youth League in the lively and creative performance of its work to suit the characteristics and needs of young people, and give full play to the League's role as a shock force and as a bridge linking the Party with great numbers of young people. Those secretaries of League committees at or below the county level or in enterprises and institutions who are Party members may attend meetings of Party committees at the corresponding levels and meetings of their standing committees as non-voting participants.

the Youth League was mobilized to help rebuild homes and buildings. Youth Leagues hold party congresses and are organized in the same fashion as the Party itself. In most communist countries, the leader of the Young Communist League is given the title first secretary and is a member of the central committee.

In China, the youth organization was suspended during the Cultural Revolution of the late 1960s. These young communists instead were mobilized by Mao to form the core of the Red Guards. They helped implement Mao's programs and gained a reputation for their ruthlessness: they were encouraged to report their parents, relatives, or neighbors if those people were violating the spirit of the Cultural Revolution. However, in 1974, the Chinese Youth League was reestablished, and by 2002, it numbered more than 69 million and had organizations in all thirty-one provinces. By 2006, Cuba's Youth League had 604,523 members, while Vietnam's had more than one million members.

6
Communism and Other Governments ▮ ▮ ▮

COMMUNIST GOVERNMENTS SHARE many characteristics with other forms of government. However, all communist governments are authoritarian systems. Hence, communist systems are either dictatorships, in which all or most political power is in the hands of an individual, or they are oligarchies, in which a small group holds all or most authority. Politically, communist regimes typically resemble other totalitarian systems, but their economic structure is what really differentiates communist governments from other types of governments. In an effort to develop a classless society in which all citizens share equally in a nation's wealth and political power, communist governments actually created a system that constrained economic growth and concentrated political authority in the hands of elites.

COMMUNISM AND OTHER ECONOMIC SYSTEMS

All governments intervene in their economy to some extent. At one end of the spectrum are communist regimes, which attempt to control and plan all aspects of the economy. At the other end of the spectrum are free-market democracies such as the United States or the United Kingdom. Yet even the free-market economies are affected by government. For instance, taxation takes money out of the economy and the government spends it for purposes deemed important. Also, most governments operate various social welfare programs, which use taxes or fees to provide services for people who might otherwise not be able, or willing, to pay for these services. Examples of social welfare programs include education, health care, or pension systems. The major distinction between the controlled economies of the com-munist states and the free-market economies of other systems is the degree of interference by the government. Most non-communist governments endeavor to minimize their interference while communist governments traditionally have sought almost total control of the economic sphere.

With the notable exception of communism, all other government systems allow some degree of private ownership of property and wealth. For instance, even socialism, which shares many of the basic ideas of communism, including the notion of class struggle and the goal of a classless society, allows for private property and accepts private ownership of most small to medium-sized businesses and factories. In democracies, assets are protected legally and constitutionally. This provides people with an incentive to work and try to acquire wealth or property. These assets may provide a better standard of living, and they can be passed on to future generations to improve the lives of families. Consequently, people often take risks to start businesses or work long hours to gain more materials or money. This is one of the foundations of the free-market system. Because people want to gain wealth, they invest their money and resources in commerce or stock, which provides businesses with the resources to develop and market new products, goods, and services. Many authoritarian regimes do not have strong protections for wealth and this allows the regime to arbitrarily confiscate property; however, citizens continue to have an incentive to build fortunes or savings in the hope that the regime will allow private use of these assets (even if only for bribes or other illicit uses).

The Basic Flaws of Communism
Communism has two fundamental flaws: it does not provide political freedom to its citizens and it limits economic freedom. In constraining political freedom, communism is like some other systems of government. However, its limitations on economic freedom also seriously undermine people's support for communist governments and the ability of regimes to compete with noncommunist governments, especially free-market capitalist

governments. Some scholars contend that Marxism runs counter to human nature. In free-market systems, people work hard to earn a raise or a promotion. However, under communism, everyone shares equally in wealth and resources; therefore, there is no incentive to work hard. In other words, if you are paid the same whether you work diligently or lazily, why work hard? Furthermore, if you do not receive higher pay and more benefits for accepting greater responsibility as a manager or supervisor, why take the position? Because there are no economic incentives to put forth extra effort, communist regimes often relied on punishment if workers and managers failed to meet specific targets. As a result, factories or other businesses usually did whatever was defined as the minimum. Consequently, production rates in communist countries were historically lower than in noncommunist states. Communism also discourages economic innovation because planning and products are controlled by the central government. Individuals who have an idea for a new product or an interest in improving an existing good or service have a difficult time convincing the government to give them permission to develop their ideas. By the late 1980s, it was clear that communism could not compete economically with democracy. As a result, between 1989 and 1991, most of the communist countries of the world abandoned the system.

COMMUNISM IN COMPARISON

Communism shares many traits and features with other authoritarian regimes in which all or most political power is concentrated in the central government as opposed to giving control to the people (a form of government broadly known as tyranny). There are several forms of tyrannical government besides communism. Ironically, most communist revolutions were undertaken to depose tyrannical governments, especially monarchies. Nonetheless, most communist governments evolved into totalitarian regimes in which not only was all political power concentrated in the central government, but the regime tried to control all aspects of people's lives. Totalitarian regimes even attempted to control social and family life. An example of a noncommunist totalitarian regime is Germany when it was controlled by Adolf Hitler and the Nazis (1933–1945). Less rigid forms of authoritarian governments include monarchies, dictatorships, and theocracies.

Economic Control

The laws of communist countries make it clear that the government is the main source of economic planning and control. For instance, Chapter Two, Article 26, of the Vietnamese Constitution proclaims that "The State manages the national economy by means of laws, plans and policies; it makes a division of responsibilities and devolves authority to various departments and levels of the administration; the interests of individuals and collectives are brought into harmony with those of the State" (Source: Vietnam, *Constitution*, 1992). Chapter One, Article 9, of the Cuban Constitution declares that the State "directs in a planned way the national economy" (Source: Cuba, *Constitution*, 1992). By contrast, in the United States Constitution, the economic powers of the government are limited. For instance, under Article I, Section 8, Congress has the authority to "lay and collect taxes, duties, imposts and excises" and "To regulate commerce with foreign nations, and among the several states, and with the Indian tribes"—this is known as the "commerce clause" (Source: United States, *Constitution*, 1789). However, nowhere is the government given a specific right or duty to oversee the U.S. economy. Instead, a limited role for the government has evolved, based on the commerce clause and later laws and court decisions. Most modern democracies follow a similar pattern of government involvement which falls far short of the five-year plans of the communist states.

Monarchies

Historically, monarchies have been the most common form of government. Monarchies are governments in which political power is concentrated in the hands of an individual, known as a king, emperor, or sheikh. Many monarchs claim that their power comes directly from God in what is known as the divine right of kings. Since the power is divine, people have no authority to try to limit the power of the monarchy. This power is transferred to a relative, usually the oldest child (most commonly, the oldest male), upon the death of the monarch. There are few real monarchies left in the world, although Great Britain, several European states, and Japan continue to have ceremonial monarchs whose power is limited by law (these are known as constitutional monarchies). The remaining monarchies include states such as Jordan, Kuwait, Oman, Qatar, Morocco, Saudi Arabia, and Swaziland. In the Pacific, Brunei and Tongo are also monarchies, as are Nepal and Bhutan in Asia. Like monarchies, many communist regimes concentrate power in the hands of a single individual. In several communist countries power even passed from one dictator to the next, as was common among monarchies. In North Korea, following the death of Premier Kim Il-sung in 1994, his son, Kim Jong-il became the country's leader. The development of a cult of personality in communist states was also seen as paralleling monarchial systems.

Dictatorships

Dictatorships are ruled by a single individual. Unlike monarchies, dictatorships are not based on inherited power and few dictators base their claim to power on the divine right of kings. Instead, dictators usually base their claim to political legitimacy on vague notions that they are a representative of the people or of a specific cause. The majority of communist regimes are dictatorial in nature. Like other dictators, communist leaders are not chosen through elections, but come to power through secret bargaining or military action. Also, like other dictatorships, communist governments rely on force to stay in power. As noted before, opponents of communist regimes face torture, exile, and other forms of punishment for simply disagreeing with the government. Many scholars assert that some communist states, such as North Korea, are simply dictatorships that use the title "communist" as propaganda to justify actions and policies to the outside world and to their own people.

Theocracy

A theocracy is a government based on religious principles or doctrine. Ancient governments in Greece or Rome would be examples of theocracy. In these cases, law and religion were intertwined and often leaders were believed to be divine. In the modern world, some governments in the Islamic world are theocracies. Their legal and political systems are based on Sharia (Islamic law). Many theocracies combine religious doctrine with authoritarian regimes. There is no separation of church and state (as is common in democracies) and therefore a violation of law is also a violation of religious beliefs. Also, theocracies often do not practice religious tolerance and instead suppress other faiths or beliefs. Theocracy and communism are incompatible since communist regimes are officially atheist. Many communist regimes brutally repressed various religious denominations and confiscated church property, while forbidding public demonstrations of faith. However, in some cases, the communist regimes have adopted religious imagery as a propaganda tool and some communist leaders have used religious themes in their creation of a cult of personality. For instance, Stalin used religious imagery in posters, statues, and paintings, including traditional Orthodox crosses.

SOCIALISM AND DEMOCRACY

Socialism

All communist systems are also socialist, but not all socialist governments are communist. Socialism shares the same basic philosophy as communism and it evolved from the ideology of many of the same thinkers, including Owen and Fourier, as well as Marx and Engels. Both ideologies share the belief that government should control the economy and that private property is not guaranteed. While people lose these economic rights, the government compensates by providing basic social needs such as education, employment, health care, and retirement pensions. In theory, socialist governments could vary from democracies to totalitarian regimes. In practice, socialist governments have been far less restrictive and authoritarian than their communist counterparts.

Some nations, particularly in Western Europe, including Sweden or Norway, have developed a blend of socialism and democracy known as social democracy. Social democracies combine representative democracy with wide-scale government involvement in the economy. While there are private businesses and private property, the government owns all or most major industries such as transportation or mining or large-scale manufacturing. Social democracies also have high taxation to support their extensive social welfare programs. Some have asserted that social democracy is an alternate route to communism (as opposed to a proletariat revolution), but no social democracies have evolved into communist regimes.

Democracy
As noted earlier, the opposite of communism is free-market democracy. Contemporary democracy is based on the notion that people control the government. All modern democracies are representative democracies in which people elect delegates to make decisions for them and to develop and implement policy. Unlike communist systems, the legislatures of democracies usually have a high degree of political power and authority. For example, the party congress is essentially a rubber stamp for decisions made by the central committee in China. In the United States, the Congress is the source of all legislation and budget planning, which then goes to the president for approval. Democracies tend to divide political power among the different branches of government (known as separation of powers) while communist regimes concentrate political power in the country's leader or among a small group in the government.

Modern democracies usually have multiple political parties. This allows different groups of people to pursue their interests with like-minded citizens. For instance, conservative political parties like the Republican Party in the United States or the Conservative Party in Great Britain seek fewer social welfare programs, while liberal parties, such as the Democratic Party in the United States or the Labour Party in Great Britain, seek an expansion of certain social programs. Democracies use political parties as a way to allow divergent views to be expressed and debated in order to allow decisions to be made based on multiple points-of-view. Conversely, communist regimes usually allow only one party, the Communist Party, and therefore they limit dissent.

Political parties are only one of several ways in which democracies encourage dissent and debate. Modern democracies allow a high degree of religious and political freedom. People have the right, usually expressed

North Korea's Cult of Personality and Dictatorship

Kim Il-sung created a cult of personality in the Democratic People's Republic of Korea (DPRK, or North Korea). Most positive accomplishments in the country were credited directly to the leader, while any problems or failures were blamed on others or the outside world. Kim's official stature continued long after his death. In the 1998 constitution (adopted four years after Kim's death), the preamble generously praised the former leader in a manner usually reserved for religious leaders:

> The great leader Comrade Kim Il-sung made clear the fundamental idea of the Republic's external policy, expanded and developed diplomatic relations on this basis, and heightened the international prestige of the Republic. Comrade Kim Il-sung as a veteran world political leader, hewed out a new era of independence, vigorously worked for the reinforcement and development of the socialist movement and the nonaligned movement, and for world peace and friendship between peoples, and made an immortal contribution to the mankind's independent cause.
>
> Comrade Kim Il-sung was a genius ideological theoretician and a genius art leader, an ever-victorious, iron-willed brilliant commander, a great revolutionary and politician, and a great human being. Comrade Kim Il-sung's great idea and achievements in leadership are the eternal treasures of the nation and a fundamental guarantee for the prosperity and efflorescence of the DPRK.

The DPRK and the entire Korean people will uphold the great leader Comrade Kim Il-sung as the eternal President of the Republic, defend and carry forward his ideas and exploits and complete the . . . revolution under the leadership of the Workers' Party of Korea.

Political Parties

While communist countries ban opposition political parties, in most democracies the political system is based on just such groups. Many Western countries even guarantee the right to form political parties in their constitutions. For instance, in France, Title I, Article 4, of the Constitution declares that "Political parties and groups shall be instrumental in the exercise of the suffrage. They shall be freely formed and shall freely carry on their activities. They must respect the principles of national sovereignty and democracy" (Source: France, *Constitution*, 1958). In Chapter II, Article 21, of the German Constitution, the right to form parties is guaranteed, unless the parties seek to overthrow the government, in which case the German Constitutional Court decides the legality of parties in question: "1) The political parties participate in the forming of the political will of the people. They may be freely established. Their internal organization must conform to democratic principles. They have to publicly account for the sources and use of their funds and for their assets. 2) Parties which, by reason of their aims or the behavior of their adherents, seek to impair or abolish the free democratic basic order or to endanger the existence of the Federal Republic of Germany are unconstitutional. The Federal Constitutional Court decides on the question of unconstitutionality." (Source: Germany, *Constitution*, 1949.)

within a constitution, to voice their opinions and beliefs. The press has the ability to freely report on the actions of the government and officials (and to criticize the government and its policies). As discussed before, in communist states there is a significant degree of control over the press and over individuals' ability to criticize the government. This feature highlights the fact that most democracies are based on individual rights, while communist regimes are based on collective rights. The communist government does not try to empower the individual, but instead works for the common good by controlling the lives of its citizens. By contrast, democracies provide for the common good by allowing individuals the maximum amount of freedom and control over their lives.

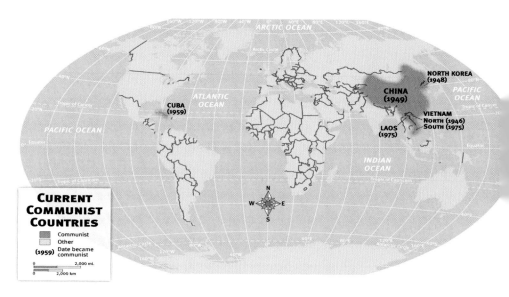

Current Communist Countries (as of 2006)

7

Communism, Today and Tomorrow

AT ONE POINT, ABOUT 25 PERCENT of the countries in the world were communist. Today only five countries are communist. The end of the Cold War in 1991 initiated an era during which most communist states transitioned away from Marxism and instead adopted other forms of government, ranging from democracy to authoritarian dictatorships. Even countries that declare themselves officially communist, including China, Cuba, North Korea, and Vietnam, have begun to shift away from the traditional principles and policies that marked communist regimes. Communism has remained popular among some segments of the population, especially in the former communist countries, and there are a number of communist parties that continue to participate in the political process, but they do so by competing with other parties rather than through a monopoly on political authority. The future of communism will be very different from its past, as the ideology continues to evolve and adapt to changes in the world.

THE END OF THE COLD WAR
The end of the Cold War demonstrated many of the problems of communism. The economies of the Soviet Union and its allies could not keep up with Western democracies and people in these nations sought greater political and economic freedom. Between 1985 and 1991, the economies of the Soviet Union and the Eastern European communist countries declined by almost 50 percent. The result was a

series of both peaceful and violent revolutions in the Soviet Union and Eastern Europe in which all the communist regimes were replaced. Communist regimes remained in place in those countries that either initiated economic reforms, as in China and Vietnam, or had especially strong political control, as was the case in Cuba and North Korea. Economic reforms in China and other communist states resulted in policies that run counter to the principles of Marxism and bring into question whether these states can still be considered communist.

China's Mixed System
One of the central notions of communism is the prohibition against private property. However, most post-Cold-War communist countries have enacted laws that allow private ownership of land and businesses. This was done to provide incentives for people to start businesses and to try to build wealth. The new measures reflected decisions by communist regimes to abandon some of the core principles of Marxism and instead adopt social democratic policies. Communist leaders realized that in order to compete with democracies and to maintain the support of their people, the regimes had to offer more economic and political freedom. Consequently, China, Vietnam, Cuba, and even North Korea abandoned some of the most repressive aspects of communist economics.

In the late 1970s, China began allowing villages and towns to take over collective enterprises such as large farms and factories. The local people were allowed to control production and decide what goods and products they make and sell. Most profits from the sale of goods and services were returned to the localities. These small, collective businesses were known as town and village enterprises (TVEs). In the 1980s, China began to allow private citizens to take over existing TVEs or start new ones and hire people so that they no longer worked for the state. By 1992, there were 8.4 million Chinese working for private businesses; by 2003, that number had increased to 49.2 million. Many of the new companies made products for export to the United States and other democracies. Because workers were paid very little compared to their Western counterparts, Chinese goods and products sold very well in other countries. In fact, many foreign firms sought to move factories and manufacturing sites to China (which the Chinese government encouraged). The experiment proved very successful. Though the Soviet economy stagnated in the

China's Constitutional Protections for Private Property

In order to protect the growing wealth of private citizens, and in an effort to attract foreign investment, on March 14, 2004, the Chinese government added a constitutional amendment to protect private property. The measure enjoyed the broad support of the Central Committee (the vote in the People's Congress was 2,863 in favor, 10 opposed, with 17 abstaining). The amendment granted citizens the right to own property and keep wages, and even gave people the right to inherit property and wealth. The measure was placed in Chapter 1, Article 13, and read, "Article 13: The state protects the right of citizens to own lawfully earned income, savings, houses and other lawful property. The state protects by law the right of citizens to inherit private property."

1980s, China's economy grew by an average of 10 percent per year (while the American economy's average annual growth was 3 percent). In addition, by 1988, China became self-sufficient in agricultural production for the first time since before World War II. Pay for Chinese workers had increased from about $200 per year in the 1970s to more than $1,000 by 2005 (this is still only about 3 percent of the average pay for an American or European worker). China's mixed system has proven to be very successful. By 2005, China was the world's fourth-largest economy, behind the United States, Japan, and Germany.

Once, all land in China was the property of the government. However, in 1988, the government enacted laws allowing land to be leased by private citizens or companies for periods ranging from forty to seventy years. Instead of paying rent, however, a lump-sum payment was required at the beginning of the lease and then the renter had more or less complete control of the property until the lease expired. Land could only be leased for a specific purpose, such as building a factory, growing crops, or building an apartment complex. Once an agreement was reached, the government allowed three years for a project to be initiated. If it was not started, the lease could be revoked with the loss of payment (the citizen or citizens who started the project could also face jail time). In 2004, China even added an amendment to its constitution that guaranteed the right to private property, something that was unheard of in a communist state.

Other Mixed Economies
Other communist countries have tried to copy China's success. Vietnam has also allowed market reforms through a program known as *doi moi* (renovation) that was launched in 1986. Doi moi broke up the large collective farms and allowed individual farmers to take possession of plots of land. The government also allowed private companies to form and invited foreign firms to establish factories and warehouses in specially designated trade zones. The result was high economic growth (8 percent per year on average between 1986 and 2003). Wages increased from about $220 per person per year to $483 by 2003. In 2001, Vietnam and the United States negotiated a trade agreement and commerce between the two countries rose to more than $6.1 billion by 2004.

During the Cold War, the Soviet Union gave billions of dollars to other communist countries. Cuba was one of the biggest beneficiaries of Soviet aid. In addition to money, the Soviet Union also provided

The erosion of communism in countries such as Vietnam allowed Western companies to enter their national markets. Here, Vietnamese schoolchildren in traditional dress enter a Kentucky Fried Chicken restaurant in Ho Chi Minh City in 2003.

Cuba with items such as consumer goods, machinery, and oil. In total, Cuba received between $4 billion and $6 billion per year from the Soviet Union. When the Cold War ended, Russia discontinued aid to its former ally. This caused severe economic problems for the regime of Fidel Castro and the economy shrank by 40 percent between 1989 and 1993. Beginning in 1990, the Cuban government created a "second economy" that included a limited number of businesses operating outside of the realm of the state-owned enterprises.

The second economy was so successful that further reforms were enacted and Cuba moved to a mixed socialist economy, like China, where some economic activities continued to be controlled by the state, while limited private companies were also allowed to operate. Under the reforms, the percentage of land under the direct control of the Cuban government declined from 78 percent to 24 percent. The number of people who were self-employed increased from 29,000 in 1990 to 168,000 by 1998. Because a large number of people had their own income and were not paid by the state, Cuba introduced an income tax, something unheard of in most communist regimes. In 1992, Cuba also reduced tariffs on foreign goods and encouraged foreign companies to invest in the island. A 1995 law known as Decree 77 even allowed foreign companies to buy property and operate businesses in Cuba. Since the 1960s, the United States has maintained an economic embargo on Cuba in an effort to force the Castro regime from power. The embargo continues to constrain Cuba's economic growth. The Cuban economy has improved since the introduction of mixed socialism, with economic growth above 5 percent per year by the late 1990s. Nevertheless, the nation remains one of the poorest countries in the Western Hemisphere.

North Korea was the last of the contemporary communist regimes to initiate economic reforms. In 2002, the government announced that workers would no longer be guaranteed a certain income level; instead they would be paid based on their performance. In addition, farmers would be allowed to sell surplus crops and livestock in unregulated farmers' markets. State-owned factories and businesses were allowed to privatize and make their own decisions about products and prices. North Korea has also been helped by increased trade with its richer, democratic neighbor, South Korea. A number of South Korean firms have established factories in North Korea, where wages are much lower. Trade between the two countries increased 250 percent between 1989 and 2004.

Decree 77 and Cuban Workers

Decree 77 opened Cuba for investments by foreign companies. It also regulated the relationship between foreign firms and Cuban workers. The measure declared that foreign companies could not directly hire Cuban workers. Instead, the corporations had to employ workers through an official employment agency. The agency charges a fee for each worker; therefore, the system provides a source of income for the government. Article 34 of the decree states:

> In totally foreign capital companies, the services of Cuban workers and foreign workers residing permanently in Cuba, with the exception of the members of the management and administrative body, shall be hired through a contract between the company and an employing entity proposed by the Ministry of Foreign Investment and Economic Cooperation, and authorized by the Ministry of Labor and Social Security.

The communist regime still plays a major role in the economy. Most North Koreans are part of the Public Distribution System (PDS), which allows people to buy a limited amount of food and other staples at a price set by the government (the price is about one-quarter of what most products cost on the open market). About 70 percent of the population is dependent on the PDS for food. The reforms have led to some improvements in the economy, but the country remains one of the poorest in the world and the United Nations estimates that as much as 20 percent of the population is malnourished.

PROBLEMS FOR POST–COLD-WAR COMMUNIST STATES

The end of the Cold War led most communist states to start the transition to other forms of government. Few people were ready for the free market, in which prices rise and fall according to the principles of supply and demand. For instance, prices on food and other basic commodities tripled in most of the countries of Eastern Europe between 1989 and 1991. Previously, the governments had regulated the cost of food, housing, and medicine. After 1989, citizens of the former Soviet states had to pay the market price for these items. In addition, people had to pay for things that had been free before, such as health care and higher education.

Many workers in the former communist states were poorly trained and used to working with obsolete equipment. Farmers were unfamiliar with the latest agricultural techniques. Furthermore, the countries had large militaries and many workers were employed in the defense industry; however, after the end of the Cold War, the new governments dramatically reduced their armed forces and eliminated many defense-related jobs. Since the communist regimes guaranteed everyone a job, workers were not used to competing for new jobs. Nor had they been exposed to merit-based performance evaluations in which they were rewarded for hard work and extra effort and in which they could be fired if they did not meet company standards.

One result of these factors was that most of the former communist countries experienced a dramatic rise in unemployment. In some countries, the increase was temporary and unemployment rates soon dropped to levels comparable to those of other Western democratic countries. By 1999, unemployment was 7.5 percent in the Czech Republic, 6.4 percent in Lithuania (in comparison, it was 6.1 percent in the United Kingdom, and in the United States it

In the countries conquered by the Soviet Union the fall of communism was met with wide-spread public celebrations. In Valmiera, Latvia, on October 1, 1990, young children touched a statue of Lenin that had been toppled following independence from the Soviet Union.

was 5.6 percent). On the other hand, some countries continued to experience high unemployment through 1999: Bulgaria, 12 percent; Russia, 12.4 percent; and Slovenia, 14.5 percent. Governments were also forced to cut back on their pension programs. On average, the former communist states cut pension payments by approximately 50 percent. Unemployment and lower pension payments resulted in dramatic increases in poverty. In 1989, there were 14 million people in the communist countries of Europe who lived below the poverty level of $4 per day. By 1996, that number had increased to 147 million, although most poverty was concentrated in a few countries. In 1989, Moldova's poverty rate was 4 percent, but by 1996 it had increased to 66 percent; Romania's increased from 6 percent to 59 percent; and Ukraine's from 2 percent to 63 percent. Meanwhile, the Czech Republic, Slovakia, and Slovenia all had poverty rates of one percent in 1989 and continue to have rates of one percent or less, while Hungary's poverty rate increased from one percent to 4 percent.

The former communist states that have performed the best since the end of the Cold War are those states that embraced democracy and the free market. The states that are fully democratic have seen their economies increase since the fall of communism. For example, Poland's economy is 21 percent larger than it was in 1989. On the other hand, states that continue to limit democracy or free trade have lagged behind. Armenia's economy is only 42 percent as large as it was in 1989, while Tajikistan's is only 43 percent as large.

The world's remaining communist countries have to balance ongoing free-market reforms and increased political freedom if the regimes are to survive. The end of the Cold War demonstrated that, when given a choice, people rejected communism as a system of government. The challenge for governments such as China or Vietnam will be to retain the positive and popular aspects of communism, such as the generous social programs, while integrating the beneficial aspects of the free-market system and allowing people more political influence through increased democracy. These countries will continue to be influenced by Marxism and some of the ideals of communism; however, new communist states are unlikely to emerge. Instead, even most communist parties have abandoned the hallmarks of former communist regimes, such as political repression, a one-party state, and the abolition of private property. Instead, most contemporary

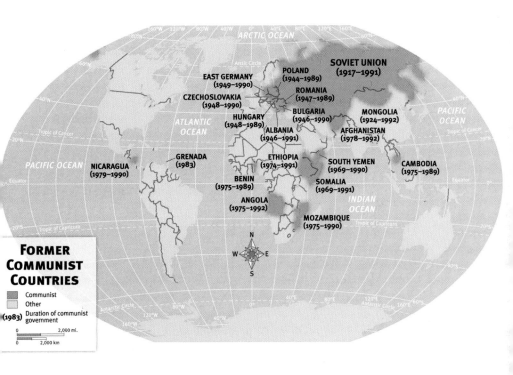

Former Communist Countries

Former Communist Parties

After the communist regimes of the Soviet Union and Eastern Europe were deposed, the former ruling parties tried to reconstitute themselves as legitimate political groups. Most went on to participate in democratic elections and in Albania, the former Communist Party was even returned to power by voters after it embraced democratic principles, including multiparty democracy, the right of private property, and a capitalist economy. The majority of the former communist parties abandoned Marxism and instead embraced social democracy and mixed economies. They advocated more social programs and a greater government role in the economy, a message that was popular with some in the former communist states. For instance, after independence, the remnants of the Communist Party in Ukraine relaunched itself as the Communist Party of Ukraine and won 66 seats in the 450-member Parliament in 2002 (in 2006, they only won 21 seats). The Communist Party in Russia splintered into several smaller communist and Marxist groups. The largest was named the Communist Party of the Russian Federation. In the 2003 elections, the party won 51 seats in the 450-seat Parliament. The most successful of the former ruling parties was the Albanian Communist Party, which renamed itself the Socialist Party. The party won elections in 1997 and remained in power until 2005. The Albanian Socialists were able to capitalize on voters' discontent with the post-communist government's economic policies. While in power, the Albanian Socialists did not try to reimpose communism. Instead they promoted social democracy and increased ties with Western Europe.

communist parties accept the right of private ownership of land and even many of the components of the free enterprise system.

No communist government ever fully implemented Marxism as that country's political or economic system. Instead, elements of Marxist ideology were combined with the ideas of revolutionary leaders such as Lenin, Mao, or Castro. In the contemporary period, the remaining regimes that declare themselves communist are moving away from those Marxist elements that were incorporated into their political systems. In the former communist states, even the successors to the Communist Party have moderated their ideology and abandoned calls for a one-party state. These parties have also embraced elements of the free-market system.

The question of succession remains problematic for communist states such as Cuba and North Korea. These states continue to be more dictatorial than communistic. If their current leaders die or lose power, the continuation of the nominally communist systems is very unlikely. In 2006, Castro was diagnosed with terminal cancer, so a succession of some sort is imminent in Cuba. The end of the twentieth century may have marked the final period of communism as a political system. Marxist ideology will continue to influence politics and economics, but it is not likely that new communist governments will come to power. Instead, elements of communism will continue to influence governments such as China or Vietnam, and continue to be manifested in the more moderate, socialist parties and governments of the world.

Communism and Other Governments

COMMUNISM	THEOCRACY	SOCIALISM
Only one legal political party (Communist Party)	Often only one legal political party	Multiple legal political parties; limited electoral freedom
No free elections; rule by a single individual or small group	Limited or no electoral freedom; rule by a single individual or small group	Rule by people through elections, although individual or small group may dominate politics
Opposition and dissent are limited or forbidden	Opposition and dissent are limited or forbidden	Opposition and dissent may be limited
No property rights	Limited property rights	Limited property rights
State-controlled economy	Government may have a significant role in economy	Government has significant role in economy
Officially no unemployment	Unemployment determined by combination of the free market and government policy	Unemployment determined by combination of the free market and government policy
No freedom of religion; limited or no civil liberties or civil rights	Religious worship limited to the state religion	May have religious freedom
Widespread social welfare programs (such as free education and health care)	Limited or no civil liberties or civil rights; social welfare programs are limited	Civil liberties and civil rights may be curtailed by government especially economic rights widespread social welfare programs (such as free education health care, and housing)

DEMOCRACY	DICTATORSHIP	MONARCHY*
Multiple legal political parties	Often only one legal political party	May have no legal political parties, or only one
Free rule by the people through elections	Limited or no electoral freedom	Limited or no electoral freedom; rule by a single individual; monarchy may be hereditary or elective
Opposition and dissent are accepted and may be encouraged	Rule by a single individual; opposition and dissent are limited or forbidden	Opposition and dissent may be limited or forbidden
Private property protected by law and constitution	Limited property rights	Limited property rights, usually inherited; monarch may claim ownership of entire kingdom
Economy determined by free market	Government may have significant role in economy	Government may have significant role in economy
Unemployment determined mainly by the free market	Unemployment determined by combination of the free market and government policy	Monarch may determine how people are to be employed; forced labor may be required
Freedom of religion	Some religious freedom, if it does not threaten the regime	Religious freedom may be allowed if it does not threaten the regime, or not, depending on ruler
Widespread and comprehensive civil liberties and civil rights; some social welfare	Limited or no civil liberties and civil rights; social welfare programs are limited	Social welfare programs may be limited

Communist Governments

Current Communist Countries
(Year the country became communist)

China (1949)
Cuba (1959)
Laos (1975)
North Korea (1948)
Vietnam (North Vietnam 1946; South Vietnam 1975)

Former Communist Countries
(Years the country was communist)

Afghanistan (1978–1992)
Albania (1946–1991)
Angola (1975–1992)
Benin (1975–1989)
Bulgaria (1946–1990)
Cambodia (1975–1989)
Czechoslovakia (1948–1990)
East Germany (1949–1990)
Ethiopia (1974–1991)

Grenada (1983)
Hungary (1948–1989)
Mongolia (1924–1992)
Mozambique (1975–1990)
Nicaragua (1979–1990)
Poland (1944–1989)
Republic of the Congo (1964–1992)
Romania (1947–1989)
Russia (1917–1991)
Somalia (1969–1991)
South Yemen (1970–1990)

Countries of the former Soviet Union (1922–1991)
(Year the country became part of the Soviet Union)

Armenia (1922)
Azerbaijan (1922)
Byelorussia (1922)
Estonia (1944)
Georgia (1936)
Kazakhstan (1925)
Kyrgyzstan (1924)
Latvia (1944)
Lithuania (1944)
Moldova (1944)
Russia (1922)
Tajikistan (1924)
Turkmenistan (1925)
Ukraine (1922)
Uzbekistan (1924)

Timeline

400–300 BCE

Early Greek philosophers emphasize communal living and public ownership of property.

30–100 CE

Some early Christians advocate rejection of wealth and endorse communal property.

1642–1651

The True Levellers (also known as the Diggers) promote communal living and land redistribution during the English Civil War.

1825

Robert Owen establishes a commune in New Harmony, Indiana.

1848

Karl Marx publishes *The Communist Manifesto.*

1917

Vladimir Lenin leads the Bolsheviks in the Russian Revolution and installs communist regime in Russia.

1928
First Five-Year Plan begins in the Soviet Union.

1945–1947
The beginnings of the Cold War appear.

1949
China becomes a communist regime.

1957
De-Stalinization programs begin in the Soviet Union following the death of Joseph Stalin.

1959
Cuba becomes the first communist state in the Western Hemisphere.

1980s
China allows limited free-market reforms.

1991
The Cold War ends; democracy spreads to many formerly communist countries.

1990s
The remaining communist countries accelerate economic and political reforms.

Notes

Chapter 1

p. 9, Laurie M. Bagby, *Political Thought: A Guide to the Classics* (Belmont, CA: Wadsworth Publishing, 2002), pp. 205–206.

p. 10, Robert V. Daniels, *The Nature of Communism* (New York: Random House, 1962), p. 3.

pp. 12–13, Karl Marx and Friedrich Engels, *The Manifesto of the Communist Party* (1848)
http://www.marxists.org/archive/marx/works/1848/communist manifesto/ch01.htm

p. 14, Keith Faulks, Ken Philips, and Alex Thompson, *Get Set for Politics* (Edinburgh: Edinburgh University Press, 2003), pp. 54–55.

p. 15, Robert L. Heilbroner, *The Worldly Philosophers: The Lives, Times and Ideas of the Great Economic Thinkers,* 6th ed. (New York: Simon and Schuster, 1986), pp. 142–144.

p. 17, Reo M. Christenson, Alan Engel, Dan Jacobs, Mostafa Rejai, and Herbert Waltzer, *Ideologies and Modern Politics,* 2nd ed. (New York: Dodd, Mead and Company, 1975), pp. 117–120.

pp. 20–21, Vladimir Lenin, *Imperialism, the Highest Stage of Capitalism* (Petrograd: Parus Publishers, 1916), http://www.marxists.org/archive/lenin/works/1916/imp-hsc/

p. 23, Arthur Cohen, *The Communism of Mao Tse-tung* (Chicago: University of Chicago, 1964), pp. 52–54.

Chapter 2

p. 24, Alan Ebenstein, *Introduction to Political Thinkers* (New York: Harcourt College Publishers, 2002), p. 6.

p. 25, Rene Coste, *Marxist Analysis and Christian Faith*, Translated by Roger A. Couture and John C. Cort (Maryknoll, NY: Orbis Books, 1985), p. 23.

p. 25, J. F. C. Harrison, *Robert Owen and the Owenites in Britain and America* (London: Routledge, 1969), p. 79.

p. 27, Robert Owen, "Address to the Citizens of New Lanark," New Lanark, January 1, 1816, http://www.robert-owen.com

p. 28, Russian Socialist Federative Soviet Republic, *Constitution*, (1918), http://www.politicsforum.org/documents/constitution_rsfsr_1918.php

p. 29, Nicholas Feodoroff, *Soviet Communists and Russian History: A Frame in Time* (Commack: Nova Science, 1997), p. 23.

pp. 31–32, Robert Service, *Stalin: A Biography* (Cambridge, MA: Harvard University Press, 2005), pp. 256–261.

pp. 32, 34, Joseph Smith and Simon Davis, *The A to Z of the Cold War* (Lanham, MD: Scarecrow Press, 2005), pp. 154–156.

p. 38, Mao Zedong, *Quotations From Mao Zedong*, (Beijing, 1966), http://www.marxists.org/reference/archive/mao/works/red-book/index.htm

p. 40, Tom Lansford, *A Bitter Harvest: US Foreign Policy and Afghanistan* (Aldershot: Ashgate, 2003), pp. 156–160.

pp. 40–41, Reo M. Christenson, Alan Engel, Dan Jacobs, Mostafa Rejai, and Herbert Waltzer, *Ideologies and Modern Politics,* 2nd ed. (New York: Dodd, Mead and Company, 1975), pp. 167–171.

Chapter 3

p. 46, Vladimir Lenin, *The State and Revolution* (Moscow, 1917), http://www.marxists.org/archive/lenin/works/1917/staterev/

p. 48, Michael Levin, *Marx, Engels, and Liberal Democracy* (New York: St. Martin's, 1989), pp. 23–27.

p. 48, Richard Hunt, *The Political Ideas of Marx and Engels.* 2 vols. (Pittsburgh: University of Pittsburgh Press, 1984), vol. 2, pp. 54–67.

p. 48, Robert V. Daniels, *The Nature of Communists* (New York: Random House, 1962), p. 89–90.

p. 50, People's Republic of China, *Constitution* [English Version], 1982, http://english.people.com.cn/constitution/constitution.html

pp. 52–53, Union of Soviet Socialist Republics, *Constitution* (1936), http://www.politicsforum.org/documents/constitution_ussr_1936.php

pp. 54–55, Edward L. Crowley, Andrew I. Lebed, and Heinrich Schulz, eds., *Party and Government Officials of the Soviet Union, 1917–1967* (Metuchen, NJ: Scarecrow Press, 1969), p. 2.

pp. 55–56, John P. Burns, ed., *The Chinese Communist Party's Nomenklatura System* (Armonk, NY: M. E. Sharpe, 1989), p. 4.

Chapter 4

p. 57, Smith and Davis, *The A to Z of the Cold War* (Lanham, MD: Scarecrow Press, 2005), p. 111.

pp. 58–59, 61, Stephane Courtois, Nicolas Werth, Karel Bartošek, Jean-Louis Panne, Jean-Louis Margolin, and Andrzej Paczkowski, *The Black Book of Communism: Crimes, Terror, Repression* (New York: Harvard University Press, 1999), p. 14.

p. 60, Nikita Khrushchev, "On the Personality Cult and Its Consequences," Moscow, February 25, 1956, http://www.historyguide. org/europe/khrush_speech.html

p. 62, Daniels, p. 83.

p. 62, Yevgenia Albats, *State Within a State: The KGB and Its Hold on Russia—Past, Present, and Future.* Translated by Catherine Fitzpatrick (New York: Farrar, Straus, and Giroux, 1995), p. 28.

p. 63, Yuri Andropov, "KGB 1967 Annual Report" (Moscow: May 6, 1968), http://www.cnn.com/SPECIALS/cold.war/episodes/21/documents/ kgb.report

p. 64, Lynne Viola, *Peasant Rebels Under Stalin: Collectivization and the Culture of Peasant Resistance* (New York: Oxford University Press, 1996), pp. 37–41.

p. 66, People's Republic of China, *Tenth Five-Year Plan for National Economic and Social Development* (Beijing, March 5, 2001), http:// www.ebeijing.gov.cn/Government/TFYPlan/t1488.htm

Chapter 5

p. 68, Christenson, Engel, Jacobs, Rejai, and Waltzer, *Ideologies and Modern Politics*, 2nd ed. (New York: Dodd, Mead and Company, 1975), p. 138.

p. 71, Robert Pastor and Qingshan Tan, "The Meaning of China's Village Elections," *The China Quarterly*, No. 162 (June 2000), p. 490.

p. 72–73, Kevin O'Brien, "Villagers, Elections and Citizenship in Contemporary China," *Modern China*, Vol. 27, no. 4 (October 2001), p. 408.

pp. 73–74, Union of Soviet Socialist Republics, *Constitution* (1977), www.departments.bucknell.edu/russian/const/1977toc.html

pp. 74, 76, Martin Ebon, *The Soviet Propaganda Machine* (New York: McGraw-Hill, 1987), pp. 97–100.

pp. 77, 80, Isabel A. Tirado, *Young Guard: The Communist Youth League, Petrograd, 1917–1920* (New York: Greenwood Press, 1988), pp. 100–111.

p. 79, People's Republic of China, *Constitution* (1982), http://english.people.com.cn/constitution/constitution.html

Chapter 6

pp. 81–82, Robert L. Heilbroner, *The Worldly Philosophers: The Lives, Times and Ideas of the Great Economic Thinkers*. 6th ed. (New York: Simon and Schuster, 1986), p. 147.

p. 84, Vietnam, *Constitution* (1992), http://coombs.anu.edu.au/~vern/van_kien/constit.html

p. 85, Cuba, *Constitution* (1992) http://www.cubanet.org/ref/dis/const_92_e.htm

p. 85, United States, *Constitution* (1789), http://www.loc.gov/rr/program/bib/ourdocs/Constitution.html

p. 86, Laurie M. Bagby, *Political Thought: A Guide to the Classics*. (Belmont, CA: Wadworth Publishing, 2002), p. 204.

p. 87, Faulks, Philips, and Thompson. *Get Set for Politics.* (Edinburgh: Edinburgh University Press, 2003), pp. 66–67.

pp. 88–89, Democratic People's Republic of Korea, *Constitution* (1998), http://www1.korea-np.co.jp/pk/061st_issue/98091708.htm

p. 91, France, *Constitution* (1958), http://www.assemblee-nationale.fr/english/8ab.asp

p. 91, Germany, *Basic Law for the Federal Republic of Germany* (1949), http://www.psr.keele.ac.uk/docs/german.htm

Chapter 7

p. 93, Martin Hart-Landsberg, and Paul Burkett, *China and Socialism: Market Reforms and Class Struggle* (New York: Review Press, 2005), p. 56.

p. 95, People's Republic of China, *Constitution* (2004), http://www.chinaembassy.se/eng/xwdt/t101768.htm

pp. 97, 99, Jorge I. Dominguez, Omar Everleny Perez Villanueva, and Lorena Bareria, eds., *The Cuban Economy at the Start of the Twenty-First Century* (Cambridge, MA: Harvard University, 2004), p. 3.

p. 99, Cuba, Decree Law 77 (1995), http://www.geo.unipr.it/~davide/cuba/economy/LAW95/index.html

p. 104, Frances Millard, *Elections, Parties, and Representation in Post-Communist Europe* (New York: Palgrave Macmillan, 2004), pp. 34–40.

All Web sites were available and accurate when sent to press.

Further Information

BOOKS

Bellamy, Edward. *Looking Backward: 2000–1887.* New York: Signet, 2000.

Blecher, Marc. *China Against the Tides: Restructuring Through Revolution, Radicalism and Reform.* London: Continuum, 2003.

Delisle, Guy. *Pyongyang: A Journey in North Korea.* New York: Farrar, Straus, and Giroux, 2005.

Dirlik, Arif. *Marxism in the Chinese Revolution.* Lanham: Rowman & Littlefield Publishers, 2005.

Gill, Graeme. *Stalinism.* New York: St. Martin's Press, 1998.

Horowitz, Irving Louis, ed. *Cuban Communism.* New Brunswick, NJ: Transaction Books, 1989.

Hunter, Maurissa. *How Communism Works.* New York: Lulu, 2005.

Jiang, Ji-Li. *Red Scarf Girl: A Memoir of the Cultural Revolution.* New York: HarperCollins, 1997.

Kort, Michael G. *China Under Communism.* Brookfield, CT: Millbrook Press, 1994.

Lankov, Andrei. *Crisis in North Korea: the Failure of De-Stalinization.* Honolulu: University of Hawaii Press, 2005.

Lawrence, Allan. *China Under Communism.* New York: Routledge, 1998.

McDermott, Kevin, and Jeremy Agnew. *The Comintern: a History of International Communism from Lenin to Stalin.* New York: St. Martin's Press, 1997.

Okey, Robin. *The Demise of Communist East Europe: 1989 in Context.* London: Arnold, 2004.

Overy, R. J. *The Dictators: Hitler's Germany and Stalin's Russia.* New York: W. W. Norton & Co., 2004.

Pantsov, Alexander. *The Bolsheviks and the Chinese Revolution, 1919–1927.* Honolulu: University of Hawaii Press, 2000.

Pipes, Richard. *Communism: A History.* New York: Modern Library, 2003.

Serge, Victor. *Midnight in the Century.* Translated by Richard Greeman. New York: Writers Publishing, 1993.

Sheldon, Garret Ward, ed. *The Encyclopedia of Political Thought.* New York: Facts On File, 2001.

Shlapentokh, Vladimir. *A Normal Totalitarian Society: How the Soviet Union Functioned and How it Collapsed.* Armonk, NY: M.E. Sharpe, 2001.

WEB SITES

Communism.org
A comprehensive site about communism that contains numerous links and information on the political ideology, including a section of frequently asked questions about communism.
http://www.communism.org

Freedom House
In annual reports, Freedom House ranks countries according to their level of individual and governmental freedom. It also details the political and civil rights in all countries and issues special reports on contemporary issues.
http://www.Freedomhouse.org

In Defense of Marxism
A Web site that details and explains the main points of Marxism. The site rebuts many of the criticisms often directed at Marxism. It has links to sites around the world and presents contemporary news and video on Marxist themes.
http://www.marxist.com

Leftist Parties of the World
A constantly updated site which provides information on communist, socialist, and Marxist political parties from all over the world, including material about their goals, leadership, and history.
http://www.broadleft.org

Marxist Internet Archive
A Web site devoted to Marxism that presents information on political theory, as well as a list of biographies and materials on major Marxist writers and theorists. It also has a history section and an online encyclopedia on Marxism.
http://www.marxists.org

Victims of Communism
Maintained by the Victims of Communism Memorial Foundation, this highly critical site provides detailed information and stories about the human costs and losses in communist regimes.
http://www.victimsofcommunism.org

All Web sites were accurate and available when sent to press.

Bibliography

Albats, Yevgenia. *State Within a State: The KGB and Its Hold on Russia—Past, Present, and Future.* Translated by Catherine Fitzpatrick. New York: Farrar, Straus and Giroux, 1995.

Andropov, Yuri. "KGB 1967 Annual Report." Moscow: May 6, 1968, http://www.cnn.com/SPECIALS/cold.war/episodes/21/documents/kgb.report

Bagby, Laurie M. *Political Thought: A Guide to the Classics.* Belmont, CA: Wadsworth Publishing, 2002.

Burns, John P., ed. *The Chinese Communist Party's Nomenklatura System.* Armonk, NY: M. E. Sharpe, 1989.

Christenson, Reo M., Alan Engel, Dan Jacobs, Mostafa Rejai, and Herbert Waltzer. *Ideologies and Modern Politics.* 2nd ed. New York: Dodd, Mead and Company, 1975.

Cohen, Arthur. *The Communism of Mao Tse-tung.* Chicago: University of Chicago, 1964.

Coste, Rene. *Marxist Analysis and Christian Faith.* Translated by Roger A. Couture and John C. Cort. Maryknoll, NY: Orbis Books, 1985.

Courtois, Stephane, Nicolas Werth, Karel Bartošek, Jean-Louis Panne, Jean-Louis Margolin and Andrzej Paczkowski. *The Black Book of Communism: Crimes, Terror, Repression.* New York: Harvard University Press, 1999.

Crowley, Edward L., Andrew I. Lebed, and Heinrich Schulz, eds. *Party and Government Officials of the Soviet Union, 1917–1967.* Metuchen, NJ: Scarecrow Press, 1969.

Cuba. *Constitution.* 1992, http://www.cubanet.org/ref/dis/const_92_e.htm

Cuba. Decree Law 77. 1995, http://www.geo.unipr.it/~davide/cuba/economy/LAW95/index.html

Daniels, Robert V. *The Nature of Communism.* New York: Random House, 1962.

Democratic People's Republic of Korea, *Constitution.* 1998, http://www1.korea-np.co.jp/pk/061st_issue/98091708.htm

Dominguez, Jorge I., Omar Everleny Perez Villanueva, and Lorena Bareria, eds. *The Cuban Economy at the Start of the Twenty-First Century.* Cambridge, MA: Harvard University, 2004.

Ebenstein, Alan. *Introduction to Political Thinkers.* New York: Harcourt College Publishers, 2002.

Ebon, Martin. *The Soviet Propaganda Machine.* New York: McGraw-Hill, 1987.

Faulks, Keith, Ken Philips, and Alex Thompson. *Get Set for Politics.* Edinburgh: Edinburgh University Press, 2003.

Feodoroff, Nicholas. *Soviet Communists and Russian History: A Frame in Time.* Commack, NY: Nova Science, 1997.

France. *Constitution*. 1958, http://www.assemblee-nationale.fr/english/8ab.asp

Germany. *Basic Law for the Federal Republic of Germany*. 1949, http://www.psr.keele.ac.uk/docs/german.htm

Harrison, J. F. C. *Robert Owen and the Owenites in Britain and America*. London: Routledge, 1969.

Hart-Landsberg, Martin, and Paul Burkett. *China and Socialism: Market Reforms and Class Struggle*. New York: Review Press, 2005.

Heilbroner, Robert L. *The Worldly Philosophers: The Lives, Times and Ideas of the Great Economic Thinkers*. 6th ed. New York: Simon and Schuster, 1986.

Hunt, Richard. *The Political Ideas of Marx and Engels*. 2 vols. Pittsburgh: University of Pittsburgh Press, 1984.

Khrushchev, Nikita. "On the Personality Cult and Its Consequences." Moscow: February 25, 1956, http://www.historyguide.org/europe/khrush_speech.html

Lansford, Tom. *A Bitter Harvest: US Foreign Policy and Afghanistan*. Aldershot: Ashgate, 2003.

Lenin, Vladimir. *Imperialism, the Highest Stage of Capitalism*. Petrograd: Parus Publishers, 1916, http://www.marxists.org/archive/lenin/works/1916/imp-hsc

Lenin, Vladimir. *The State and Revolution*. Moscow, 1917, http://www.marxists.org/archive/lenin/works/1917/staterev

Levin, Michael. *Marx, Engels, and Liberal Democracy*. New York: St. Martin's, 1989.

Marx, Karl, and Friedrich Engels. *The Manifesto of the Communist Party*. 1848. http://www.marxists.org/archive/marx/works/1848/communist manifesto/ch01.htm

Millard, Frances. *Elections, Parties, and Representation in Post-Communist Europe.* New York: Palgrave Macmillan, 2004.

O'Brien, Kevin. "Villagers, Elections and Citizenship in Contemporary China." *Modern China.* vol. 27, no. 4 (October 2001).

Owen, Robert. "Address to the Citizens of New Lanark." New Lanark, January 1, 1816, http://www.robert-owen.com/

People's Republic of China. *Constitution* [English Version]. 1982, http://english.people.com.cn/constitution/constitution.html

People's Republic of China. *Constitution.* 2004, http://www.chinaembassy.se/eng/xwdt/t101768.htm

People's Republic of China. *Tenth Five-Year Plan for National Economic and Social Development.* Beijing: March 5, 2001, http://www.ebeijing.gov.cn/Government/TFYPlan/t1488.htm

Russian Socialist Federative Soviet Republic. *Constitution.* 1918. http://www.politicsforum.org/documents/constitution_rsfsr_1918.php

Service, Robert. *Stalin: A Biography.* Cambridge, MA: Harvard University Press, 2005.

Smith, Joseph, and Simon Davis. *The A to Z of the Cold War.* Lanham, MD: Scarecrow Press, 2005.

Tirado, Isabel A. *Young Guard: The Communist Youth League, Petrograd, 1917–1920.* New York: Greenwood Press, 1988.

Union of Soviet Socialist Republics. *Constitution.* 1936, http://www.politicsforum.org/documents/constitution_ussr_1936.php

Union of Soviet Socialist Republics. *Constitution.* 1977, http://www.departments.bucknell.edu/russian/const/1977toc.html

United States. *Constitution.* 1789, http://www.loc.gov/rr/program/bib/ourdocs/Constitution.html

Vietnam. *Constitution.* 1992, http://coombs.anu.edu.au/~vern/van_kien/constit.html

Viola, Lynne. *Peasant Rebels Under Stalin: Collectivization and the Culture of Peasant Resistance.* New York: Oxford University Press, 1996.

Zedong, Mao. *Quotations from Mao Zedong.* Beijing: 1966, http://www.marxists.org/reference/archive/mao/works/red-book/index.htm

All Web sites were available and accurate when sent to press.

Index

Page numbers in **boldface** are illustrations, tables, and charts.

About the Author

Tom Lansford is the assistant dean of the College of Arts and Letters and an associate professor of political science at the University of Southern Mississippi. He is the author or editor of more than than twenty books on politics, government, and international relations. *Communism* and *Democracy* in the Political Systems of the World series are his first books for Marshall Cavendish Benchmark. Dr. Lansford is also the author of more than one hundred encyclopedic entries, book chapters, and short essays. He lives in Long Beach, Mississippi.